50 Walks

# WATERSIDE

D0813160

30130 150539962

Produced by AA Publishing
© Automobile Association Developments Limited 2007
Illustrations © Automobile Association Developments Limited 2007

Published by AA Publishing (a trading name of Automobile
Association Developments Limited, whose registered office is Fanum
House, Basing View, Basingstoke, Hampshire RG21 4EA;
registered number 1878835)

 This product includes mapping data licensed
from Ordnance Survey® with the permission of
the Controller of Her Majesty's Stationery
Office.© Crown copyright 2007. All rights
reserved. Licence number 100021153

ISBN 978-0-7495-5551-1

A03033e

A CIP catalogue record for this book is available
from the British Library.

The contents of this book are believed correct at the time of printing.
Nevertheless, the publishers cannot be held responsible for any errors
or omissions or for changes in the details given in this book or for
the consequences of any reliance on the information it provides. We
have tried to ensure accuracy in this book, but things do change and
we would be grateful if readers would advise us of any inaccuracies
they may encounter.

We have taken all reasonable steps to ensure that these walks are
safe and achievable by walkers with a realistic level of fitness.
However, all outdoor activities involve a degree of risk and the
publishers accept no responsibility for any injuries caused to
readers whilst following these walks. For more advice on walking
safely see opposite.

Some of the walks may appear in other AA publications.

Visit the AA Publishing website at www.theAA.com

Colour reproduction by Keene Group, Andover
Printed in China by Everbest Printing

# Walking in Safety

All these walks are suitable for any reasonably fit person, but less experienced walkers should try the easier walks first. Route finding is usually straightforward, but you will find that an Ordnance Survey map is a useful addition to the route maps and descriptions.

**Risks**

Although each walk here has been researched with a view to minimising the risks to the walkers who follow its route, no walk in the countryside can be considered to be completely free from risk. Walking in the outdoors will always require a degree of common sense and judgement to ensure that it is as safe as possible.

- Be particularly careful on cliff paths and in upland terrain, where the consequences of a slip can be very serious.

- Remember to check tidal conditions before walking on the seashore.

- Some sections of route are by, or cross, busy roads. Take care and remember traffic is a danger even on minor country lanes.

- Be careful around farmyard machinery and livestock, especially if you have children with you.

- Be aware of the consequences of changes in the weather and check the forecast before you set out. Carry spare clothing and a torch if you are walking in the winter months. Remember the weather can change very quickly at any time of the year, and in moorland and heathland areas, mist and fog can make route finding much harder. Don't set out in these conditions unless you are confident of your navigation skills in poor visibility. In summer remember to take account of the heat and sun; wear a hat and carry spare water.

- On walks away from centres of population you should carry a whistle and survival bag. If you do have an accident requiring the emergency services, make a note of your position as accurately as possible and dial 999.

Legend & map

# Legend

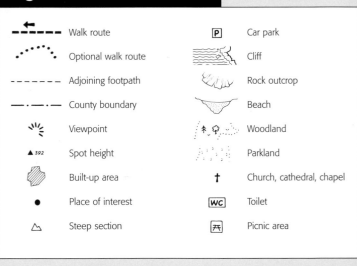

| | | | |
|---|---|---|---|
|  | Walk route | P | Car park |
| | Optional walk route | | Cliff |
| | Adjoining footpath | | Rock outcrop |
| | County boundary | | Beach |
| | Viewpoint | | Woodland |
| ▲ 392 | Spot height | | Parkland |
| | Built-up area | † | Church, cathedral, chapel |
| ● | Place of interest | WC | Toilet |
| △ | Steep section | 禾 | Picnic area |

# locator map

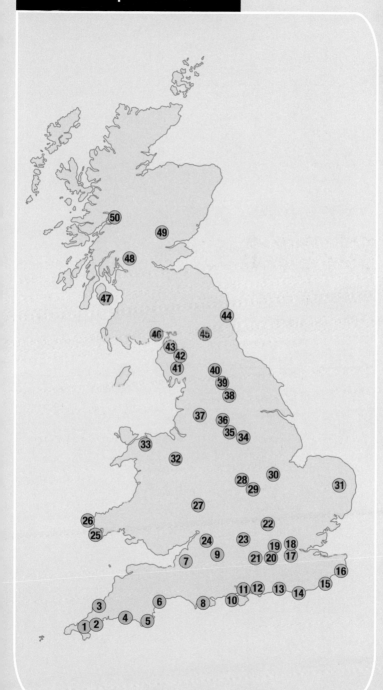

Contents

# Contents

Contents

**Rating:** Each walk is rated for its relative difficulty compared to the other walks in this book. Walks marked 🚶🚶 🚶🚶 🚶🚶 are likely to be shorter and easier with little total ascent. The hardest walks are marked 🚶🚶 🚶🚶 🚶🚶 .

**Walking in Safety:** For advice and safety tips see page 3.

# Introduction

There's something about being near water which fascinates people. This love affair has been expressed in various ways, from John Glover-Kind's jovial 1909 song, 'I do Like to be Beside the Seaside', to Kenneth Grahame's lovable character Ratty, who a year earlier in the classic *The Wind in the Willows*, described 'The River' to the Mole: "It's my world, and I don't want any other. What it hasn't got is not worth having, and what it doesn't know is not worth knowing."

Britain is extraordinarily fortunate in its waterside delights. Our 6,000 miles of infinitely varied and beautiful coastline – the longest in Europe – has exerted a profound influence on the nation's history and the character of its people. And our 1,500 river systems have played a fundamental role in the economic, social and cultural life of the country. Add to that the 1,500 man-made miles of navigable canals which are left and the wealth of both natural lakes and reservoirs and you can see why we are spoilt for choice when it comes to waterside rambles.

And there are few more pleasant ways of enjoying these wonders than taking a stroll along the coast or beside a river, reservoir, lake or canal. In these 50 family walks we sample the best of British waterside walking, from the southernmost tip of Cornwall to the Highlands of Scotland.

Among them you can enjoy the spectacular 6¾ mile (10.9km) walk along Dorset's 140 million-year-old World Heritage Jurassic Coast, from Lulworth Cove to Durdle Door and beyond in Walk 8. This is a roller-coaster of a walk which, in addition to the scenic highlights of scallop-shaped Lulworth Cove and the soaring natural flying buttress of Durdle Door, includes the option to take in the Fossil Forest off Little Bindon to the east of Lulworth. You can taste the delights of the cliff-top Pembrokeshire Coast National Trail on Walk 26, around St David's Head.

Of course, not all of Britain's coastal scenery consists of soaring cliffs and spectacular beaches. Walk 15, for example, shows how Rye Harbour on the gentle Sussex coast, has been the first line of defence against invaders since Napoleonic times. This easy, two-hour, 4½ mile (7.2km) walk on level paths takes you past an early 19th-century Martello Tower and then through the Rye Harbour Nature Reserve, where in summer you might catch sight of migrant little terns.

At the other end of the country, the short, 2½ mile (4km) linear walk up the Himalayan-scale Nevis Gorge (Walk 50) in the shadow of Britain's highest mountain (Ben Nevis, 4,406ft/1,344m) gives you a taste of walking on the wild side. A steep ascent along a well-built path leads to the reward of the sight of the spectacular Steall Falls, which tumble an impressive 300 feet (91m) from the Allt Coire a Mhail above, in a classic example of a hanging valley left behind by an Ice Age glacier. Other hill-walking excursions include some of the best of the English Lakes, round Elter Water and Loughrigg Tarn, Ullswater, and on Walla Crag.

If you prefer your walking to be on the flat, try the 5 mile (8km) stroll around the lakes of the Cotswold Water Park. These former gravel pits were flooded to create a haven for wildlife, anglers and water sport enthusiasts, and show how Nature can heal the scars of industry.

At the other end of the Thames, the 4¼ mile (6.8km) stroll along the towpaths and banks of the River Lea near Bromley-by-Bow in London is another example of how an industrial landscape has been transformed into a peaceful haven for walkers.

Although obviously man-made, the reservoirs which supply water to our industrial cities can often soften a harsh moorland scene. A good example is the series which flood the Dove Stones valley near Oldham. Walk 36 is a strenuous 8-mile (12.9km) moorland hike which passes the Dovestone, Yeoman Hey and Greenfield Reservoirs and ascends Birchen Clough, before passing along the moorland edge to return.

More gentle is the stroll around the Hambleton peninsula which extends into Rutland Water – one of the largest artificial lakes in western Europe. The 3,100 acre (1,255ha) reservoir is now the home to over 250 species of birds – including the introduced fish-eating osprey.

## Using this Book

### Information panels
A panel for each walk shows its relative difficulty, the distance and total amount of ascent. An indication of the gradients you will encounter is shown by the rating ▲▲▲ (no steep slopes) to **▲▲▲** (several very steep slopes).

### Maps
Each of the 50 walks in this book has its own map, with the walk route clearly marked with a hatched line. Some can be extended by following an extra section of route marked with a dotted line, but for reasons of space, instructions for the extensions are not given in the text. The minimum time suggested for the walk is for reasonably fit walkers and doesn't allow for stops. Each walk has a suggested large-scale OS map which should be used in conjunction with the walk route map. Laminated aqua3 maps are longer lasting and water resistant.

### Start Points
The start of each walk is given as a six-figure grid reference prefixed by two letters indicating which 100km square of the National Grid it refers to. You'll find more information on grid references on most Ordnance Survey maps.

### Dogs
We have tried to give dog owners useful advice about how dog friendly each walk is. Please respect other countryside users. Keep your dog under control, especially around livestock, and obey local bylaws and other dog control notices.

### Car Parking
Many of the car parks suggested are public, but occasionally you may find you have to park on the roadside or in a lay-by. Please be considerate when you leave your car, ensuring that access roads or gates are not blocked and that other vehicles can pass safely.

**Walk 1**

# A Waterside Walk by the Fal Estuary

*From Mylor Churchtown to Flushing in a quiet peninsula world still dominated by ships and sails.*

| | |
|---|---|
| •DISTANCE• | 4 miles (6.4km) |
| •MINIMUM TIME• | 3hrs |
| •ASCENT / GRADIENT• | 164ft (50m) ▲ ▲ ▲ |
| •LEVEL OF DIFFICULTY• | 🚶 🚶🚶 🚶🚶 |
| •PATHS• | Good paths throughout. Wooded section to Trelew Farm is often very wet, 7 stiles |
| •LANDSCAPE• | Wooded peninsula flanked by river estuaries and creeks |
| •SUGGESTED MAP• | aqua3 OS Explorer 105 Falmouth & Mevagissey |
| •START / FINISH• | Grid reference: SW 820352 |
| •DOG FRIENDLINESS• | Dogs on lead through grazed areas. |
| •PARKING• | Mylor Churchtown car park |
| •PUBLIC TOILETS• | Mylor Churchtown and Flushing |

## BACKGROUND TO THE WALK

The inner estuary of the River Fal, the Carrick Roads, is reputedly the third largest natural harbour in the world. It has welcomed all manner of vessels, from Tudor warships to fishing fleets, to modern cargo vessels and oil rigs and a growing number of yachts. Part of the long maritime heritage of the Fal belongs to the Post Office Packet Service that was responsible for communications throughout the British Empire. The Packet Service was based in the Fal from 1689 to 1850. It was a glorious and freebooting period of British seafaring. Fast Packet vessels ran south to Spain and Portugal and then on to the Americas. The Packet sailors were notorious for their opportunism and many a Packet ship returned from a trip with more than half its cargo as contraband goods. The main Packet base was at Falmouth, but Mylor was a servicing and victualling yard for the Packet boats and many of the Packet captains lived at Flushing in what was effectively maritime suburbia.

### Leisure Sailing

At Mylor today, maritime traditions are as strong as ever, as far as leisure sailing goes. Boatyards still bustle with work and local sailing clubs thrive. A gold medal winner in sailing at the 2000 Olympics in Australia, Ben Ainslie, learned many of his skills as a Laser dinghy sailor in these waters and today every creek and inlet of the Fal is dense with sailing and leisure craft. Modern Flushing is an exquisitely peaceful backwater, within shouting distance of bustling Falmouth, but with the river between.

### Wooded Valley

The walk takes you from Mylor along the shores of the blunt headland between Mylor Creek and the Penryn River and on to Flushing, in full view of Falmouth docks and waterfront. Flushing is a charming enclave of handsome houses, many with distinctly Dutch features. At Point ④ on the walk, note the plaque opposite, commemorating the Post Office Packet service. From Flushing you turn inland and on to a delightful old track that runs down a wooded valley to the tree-shrouded waters of Mylor Creek from where quiet lanes lead back to St Mylor Church. Here in a churchyard that resonates with maritime history, stands the Ganges Memorial, a commemoration of 53 youngsters who died, mainly of disease, on the famous Royal Naval training ship HMS *Ganges* that was based at Mylor from 1866 to 1899.

## Walk 1 Directions

① From the car park entrance at **Mylor Churchtown**, turn right to the start of a surfaced walkway, signposted to Flushing. Follow the walkway, then, by the gateway of a house, bear left along a path signposted to **Flushing**. Pass in front of **Restronguet Sailing Club**, go up some steps and turn left along the coast path.

② Follow the path round **Penarrow Point** and continue round **Trefusis Point**. Reach a gate and granite grid stile by a wooden shack at **Kilnquay Wood**. Continue to a lane.

### WHERE TO EAT AND DRINK

Half-way through the route, at Flushing, there are two good pubs, the **Seven Stars Inn** and the **Royal Standard Inn**. At Mylor Bridge there is a restaurant on the waterfront, the **HMS *Ganges* Restaurant**.

**Walk 1**

**WHILE YOU'RE THERE** ⓘ
Visit the Parish **Church of St Mylor** and the **HMS** *Ganges* **Memorial** in the churchyard. The church has a gnomic tower and a campanile, a separate tower, houses the church bells. The *Ganges* was a famous Victorian training ship that moved to Harwich in 1899 and became a shore establishment in 1905. The original *Ganges* was a three-masted sailing gunship, built in Bombay and the last of its kind to sail round Cape Horn.

③ Follow the surfaced lane round left, then go right through a gap beside a gate and continue along a public road. Where the road drops down towards the water's edge, bear right up a surfaced slope to reach the delightful grassy area of the '**Bowling Green**'. (Strictly no dog fouling please.) Continue past a little pavilion and toilets and go down a surfaced walkway, then turn left by a junction and signpost into Flushing.

④ Turn right at a street junction and go along **Trefusis Road** past the **Seven Stars Inn**. At a junction by the **Royal Standard Inn**, keep right past the **Post Office** and go up **Kersey Road**. At the top of the road, by **Orchard Vale**, go left up steps, signposted '**Mylor Church**'. Cross a stile and keep to the field edge to reach an isolated house and to a stile made of granite bollards.

⑤ In a few paces go right through a gate then turn left over a cattle grid and follow the drive to a public road, **Penarrow Road**. Cross with care, and go down the road opposite for 30yds (27m), then go right down steps and on down the field edge. Keep straight ahead where the field edge bends left, and enter shady woods.

⑥ Enter the woodland and keep right at a junction to follow a rocky path that is often a mini stream after heavy rainfall. Go through a gate, keep left at a junction then cross a proper stream. Go through a tiny gate and turn right down a farm track to reach a surfaced lane at **Trelew**.

⑦ Turn right along the lane, passing an old water pump. When you get to a slipway, keep ahead along the unsurfaced **Wayfield Road**. Continue along between granite posts and on to join the public road into **Mylor Churchtown**. Cross the road with care (this is a blind corner) and go through the churchyard of **St Mylor Church** (please note, the path through the churchyard is not a public right of way). Turn right when you reach the waterfront to find the **car park**.

**WHAT TO LOOK FOR** ⓘ
The wooded sections of the walk are composed mainly of deciduous trees. Unlike conifer woods, these diverse environments support numerous flowering plants amidst their damp, tangled, humus-rich undergrowth. Look for the pink and red flowers of herb robert and campion and the starry white blooms of greater stitchwort. This latter plant was believed to have curative properties in earlier times; it was ground into a paste and applied to boils and sores. Children in Cornwall were once warned not to touch stitchwort at night or they would become 'pixie-led' and lost in the woods.

# St Anthony's Guns and Guiding Lights

*A walk on the beautiful Roseland Peninsula, visiting an ancient church, a lighthouse, and an old gun battery.*

| | |
|---|---|
| •DISTANCE• | 6½ miles (10.4km) |
| •MINIMUM TIME• | 4hrs |
| •ASCENT / GRADIENT• | 230ft (70m) ▲▲ ▲ ▲ |
| •LEVEL OF DIFFICULTY• | 🚶🚶 🚶🚶 🚶🚶 |
| •PATHS• | Excellent coastal and creekside footpaths. May be muddy in places during wet weather, 12 stiles |
| •LANDSCAPE• | Picturesque headland with open coast on one side and sheltered tidal creek and estuary on the other |
| •SUGGESTED MAP• | aqua3 OS Explorer 105 Falmouth & Mevagissey |
| •START / FINISH• | Grid reference: SW 848313 |
| •DOG FRIENDLINESS• | Dogs on lead through grazed areas |
| •PARKING• | National Trust St Anthony Head car park. Can be busy in summer. There is alternative parking on the route at Porth Farm (Point ③, SW 868329) |
| •PUBLIC TOILETS• | St Anthony Head car park and Porth Farm car park |

## BACKGROUND TO THE WALK

Headlands demand attention. They stick their necks out into seaways, guard the entrance to river estuaries, and can spell disaster to careless seagoers. St Anthony Head on the east side of the Falmouth Estuary deserves more attention than most. It lies at the tip of the most southerly promontory of the beautiful Roseland Peninsula and was always of strategic importance. There was a gun battery on St Anthony Head from the early 19th century until 1957, its purpose being to defend the key port of Falmouth. The lighthouse on the Head was built in 1834. One of its main purposes is to warn vessels of the highly dangerous reefs known as the Manacles that lie offshore from Porthoustock below St Keverne.

As early as 1805, guns were positioned on St Anthony Head to cover the approaches to Falmouth. By the end of the 19th century the headland had been transformed into a formidable gun battery that remained either active or in readiness until after the Second World War. By 1957 Coastal Artillery was discontinued and the St Anthony Battery was stripped of its ordnance. The site came into the care of the National Trust in 1959.

### Towan Beach

The route of this walk starts from above the lighthouse and makes a circuit of the narrow peninsula behind St Anthony Head. The route encompasses the contrasting water worlds of the open sea and the enclosed Percuil River and tidal inlet of Porth Creek. The first part of the walk lies along the breezy east side of the peninsula. The path soon passes above the cliff-fringed Porthbeor Beach. Another ½ mile (800m) takes you to the splendid Towan Beach within its sheltering bay. From the settlement of Porth, above the beach, the route heads inland and follows the opposite side of the peninsula. Leafy paths wind along the wooded shores of Porth Creek and the Percuil River to pass the 19th-century Place House and St Anthony's Church. Beyond the church a more open coast is reached. On the opposite headland stands the village of St Mawes and across the wider estuary lies busy Falmouth. Here you regain the scent and sound of the sea. The path now takes you south along the sea's edge back to St Anthony Head, where you can visit the lighthouse at certain times and divert also to the old Observation Post on the high ground above (see While You're There).

## Walk 2 Directions

① Leave the St Anthony Head car park at its far end and keep straight ahead along a surfaced lane past a row of holiday cottages on the left. Follow the coast path, running parallel with the old military road alongside **Drake's Downs**, to where the coast path passes above

**Porthbeor Beach** at a junction with the beach access path.

② Follow the coast path round **Porthmellin Head** and **Killigerran Head** to reach **Towan Beach**. At the junction with the beach access path, turn left and inland. Bear off left before a gate and go through a roofed passageway, there are toilets on the left, to reach a road.

Walk 2

③ Go straight across the road and through a gapway, signed for 'Porth Farm', then go down a surfaced drive. Turn into the entrance to the National Trust car park, then bear off left along a grassy path signposted 'Place via Percuil River'. Soon cross a footbridge, then turn right. Follow the edge of Froe Creek to a stile into the woods, then follow a path alongside Porth Creek and through Drawler Plantation, ignoring side paths to 'Bohortha'.

④ Pass a small jetty where the St Mawes ferry picks up passengers. Continue to a kissing gate and onto the road end in front of Place House. Go left along the road and uphill.

⑤ Turn right and cross a stile by a red gate, signposted 'Church of St Anthony and St Anthony Head'. Follow the path past the gravestones to the church. Keep dogs under control here. Go up the steps opposite the church door and follow a shady path uphill. Bear right, then, at a T-junction with a track, turn right. Follow the track ahead then, at a bend, bear off to the left. Go over a stile

**WHILE YOU'RE THERE**

St Anthony Lighthouse is open to visitors at certain times, depending on lighthouse duties. Halfway up the path between lighthouse and car park, you can divert to the right along a path that takes you to a preserved Battery Observation Post and to a bird hide overlooking the cliffs at Zone Point.

by a gate, then follow the edge of the field uphill. Cross over a stile, (there's a seat to your left) and keep straight ahead and downhill until you get to the water's edge.

⑥ Turn left and follow the coast path around Carricknath Point. Just past Great Molunan Beach, cross a causewayed dam above a small quay, then, at a junction, keep right and follow the coast path signs. At a junction with a surfaced track coming down from the left, keep straight ahead to St Anthony Lighthouse.

⑦ Return to the junction and climb the steep, surfaced track to reach the car park. Halfway up, another track leads off right to the preserved Battery Observation Post and to the bird hide above Zone Point.

**WHAT TO LOOK FOR**

In the sheltered waters of Porth Creek and the Percuil River, look out for the heron and other wading birds such as curlews and oyster catchers. The latter is unmistakable because of its glossy black breast and back feathers, its snow-white underparts and its distinctive orange bill. Around St Anthony Head, the various viewpoints, such as the Battery Observation Post and the bird hide at Zone Point, offer opportunities for spotting seabirds such as the fulmar, cormorant, kittiwake, and gannet. The gannet's beak is made of bone and the bird's skull is exceptionally strong to help cushion the explosive impact it makes when diving at speed into the sea in pursuit of fish. However, gannets eventually develop poor eyesight because of repeated impact with the water and sadly many die from diving onto underground reefs that they mistake for shoals of fish.

**Walk 3**

# Along the Banks of the River Camel at Wadebridge

*A gentle walk along the famous old railway trackbed of the Camel Trail and through less-visited woodlands.*

| | |
|---|---|
| •DISTANCE• | 6 miles (9.7km) |
| •MINIMUM TIME• | 3hrs 30min |
| •ASCENT / GRADIENT• | 328ft (100m) |
| •LEVEL OF DIFFICULTY• | |
| •PATHS• | Farm and forestry tracks and well-surfaced old railway track |
| •LANDSCAPE• | Wooded riverside |
| •SUGGESTED MAP• | aqua3 OS Explorer 106 Newquay and Padstow |
| •START / FINISH• | Grid reference: SW 991722 |
| •DOG FRIENDLINESS• | Dogs should be kept under control and restrained from roaming fields and property adjacent to the Camel Trail. On lead through grazed areas and if notices indicate |
| •PARKING• | Wadebridge main car park. Small parking area at end of Guineaport Road at start of the Camel Trail |
| •PUBLIC TOILETS• | The Platt, Wadebridge |

## BACKGROUND TO THE WALK

Wadebridge is emphatically a river town. Even its name defines it as such. Before the mid-15th century the settlement on the banks of the Camel River, upstream from Padstow was known simply as 'Waed', the fording place. It was a dangerous passage across the Camel here and there were many drownings and near escapes. Eventually, in 1485, money was raised for the building of a bridge, known subsequently as 'The Bridge on Wool'. Contemporary records suggest that the foundations for the stone piers of the new bridge were actually made up of wool sacks. But another, less appealing but possibly more accurate, explanation is that the money for the bridge was earned from the lucrative wool trade of the medieval period. The bridge has 17 arches and is 320ft (98m) long. It was widened in 1847 and is recognised as being one of the finest examples of a medieval bridge in Britain.

**Famous Railway**

In the 19th century Wadebridge also acquired a famous railway, first linking the town to Bodmin in 1834 and then to Padstow in 1899. The Wadebridge to Bodmin section was built to carry sand extracted from the Camel Estuary for agricultural use to improve soil conditions. In return the railway carried china clay and granite from the quarries on Bodmin Moor for export by sea. Extending the railway line to Padstow led to the decline of Wadebridge as a port but the Padstow link also established the line as part of the great Atlantic Coast Express carrying huge numbers of holidaymakers from London and the heart of England to the Cornish seaside resorts. The journey from Bodmin through Wadebridge to Padstow was immortalised by the poet John Betjeman who described its length as 'the most beautiful train journey...'

Walk 3

## Recreational Trail

The line was closed in the 1960s. In 1980 Cornwall County Council bought the section from Boscarne Junction near Bodmin to Padstow and turned it into a recreational trail, the Camel Trail, that has subsequently been enjoyed by vast numbers of walkers, cyclists, horse riders, anglers and birdwatchers. This walk follows part of the Camel Trail, but first leads inland through deeply wooded countryside. The route climbs steadily above the Camel valley to the serene little hamlet of Burlawn before it descends into an enfolding blanket of woodland by Hustyn Mill from where it leads to Polbrock Bridge, where the River Camel and the Camel Trail cling to each other like snakes. From Polbrock Bridge you follow the Camel Trail effortlessly back to Wadebridge, in more crowded circumstances at times and sharing the experience with cyclists, yet within that same persuasive world of trees, river, and Cornish air that so enchanted Betjeman.

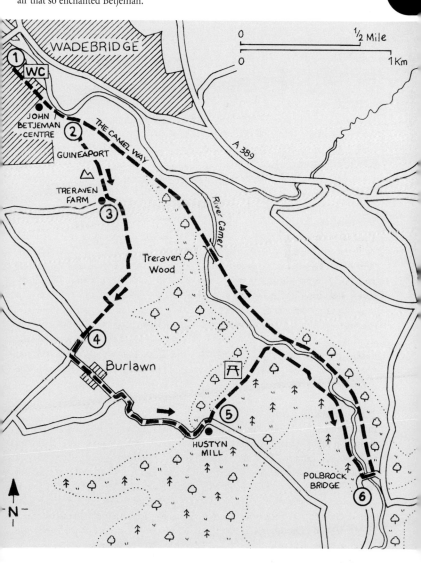

**Walk 3**

# Walk 3 Directions

① From the car parks in Wadebridge, walk along **Southern Way Road** past the **Betjeman Centre** and continue along **Guineaport Road** to the start of the **Camel Trail**. Start from here if adjacent parking is used.

> **WHERE TO EAT AND DRINK** ⓘ
> There are no refreshment outlets along the route but Wadebridge has a number of pubs, restaurants and cafés. The **Swan Hotel** in Molesworth Street, the town's main street leading to its famous bridge, does good traditional food.

② Do not follow the Camel Trail. Instead, where the road forks just past a row of houses, keep right and within a few paces, at a junction, where the road curves up to the right, keep ahead along an unsurfaced track signposted '**Public Footpath to Treraven**'. Follow the track steadily uphill. Go through a wooden gate and follow the right-hand field edge to go through another gate. Continue along a track to reach a junction with a wider track. Keep ahead and follow the track.

> **WHILE YOU'RE THERE** ⓘ
> Visit the **John Betjeman Centre** in Southern Way, Wadebridge. It's in the old railway station and contains memorabilia of the famous Poet Laureate. He was unsurpassed as a chronicler of suburbia and the countryside, and a lover of the Padstow and Wadebridge area where he had a family home. Open Monday to Friday, 10–4:30.

③ Go left in front of **Treraven Farm**, then, in about 15yds (14m), at a junction, keep right and continue along the track to reach a bend on a minor public road by a building.

④ Keep straight ahead along the road, with care, then turn left at a cross roads, signposted '**Burlawn**'. At the next junction, go left and follow the road through Burlawn. Go steeply downhill on a narrow lane overshadowed by trees.

⑤ At **Hustyn Mill**, beyond a little footbridge, turn left off the road and follow a broad woodland track. Stay on the main track to where it reaches the surfaced road at **Polbrock Bridge**.

> **WHAT TO LOOK FOR** ⓘ
> The River Camel and its flanking woods are a perfect habitat for birds. Look for goldfinch and nuthatch, amongst the trees and for heron and curlew on the river. In the spring and autumn, if you are very lucky, you may spot birds of passage such as the beautiful little egret in its snow-white plumage.

⑥ Turn left over the bridge across the **River Camel** and, in a few paces, go off left and down steps to join the **Camel Trail**. Turn left here and follow the unwavering line of the Camel Trail back to **Wadebridge**.

# The Cornish Shores of Plymouth Sound

*A walk round the Mount Edgcumbe estate on the shores of Plymouth Sound.*

| | |
|---|---|
| **•DISTANCE•** | 8 miles (12.9km) |
| **•MINIMUM TIME•** | 4hrs |
| **•ASCENT / GRADIENT•** | 328ft (100m) ▲▲▲ |
| **•LEVEL OF DIFFICULTY•** | 🚶 🚶 🚶 |
| **•PATHS•** | Good throughout. Muddy in places in wet weather, 8 stiles |
| **•LANDSCAPE•** | Wooded shoreline of tidal creek, fields, woods and coast |
| **•SUGGESTED MAP•** | aqua3 OS Explorer 108 Lower Tamar Valley & Plymouth |
| **•START / FINISH•** | Grid reference: SX 453534 |
| **•DOG FRIENDLINESS•** | Dogs on lead through grazed areas |
| **•PARKING•** | Cremyll car park. Alternatively reach Cremyll by ferry from the Plymouth side. Daily service between Admiral's Hard, Stonehouse, Plymouth and Cremyll |
| **•PUBLIC TOILETS•** | Cremyll and Kingsand |

## BACKGROUND TO THE WALK

The Mount Edgcumbe Country Park is a green oasis that flies in the face of Plymouth's crowded waterfront opposite. The two are separated by The Narrows, a few hundred yards (metres) of the 'Hamoaze', the estuary formed by the rivers Tavy, Lynher and Tamar. Mount Edgcumbe stands on the Cornish side of the river, although it was not always 'Cornish'. In Anglo Saxon times, Devon extended across the estuary as far as Kingsand, the halfway point in this walk. Today, however, Mount Edgcumbe and its waterfront settlement of Cremyll are emphatically Cornish. They stand on the most easterly extension of the Rame Peninsula, known with ironic pride by local people as the 'Forgotten Corner'. In truth Rame is one of the loveliest parts of the South West, let alone of Cornwall, and this walk takes you round the shores of the inner estuary, and then over the spine of the eastern peninsula to Kingsand, before returning to Cremyll along the open shores of Plymouth Sound.

### Empacombe

The first section of the route takes you to peaceful Empacombe, where there is a tiny harbour contained within a crescent-shaped quay. It was here, during 1706–9, that workshops servicing the building of the famous Eddystone Lighthouse were located. Behind the harbour is the Gothic facade of Empacombe House. The path follows the wooded shoreline of the tidal basin known as Millbrook Lake, then climbs steeply inland to reach Maker Church on the highest point of the peninsula. From here you wander through tiny fields to reach a track that leads in a long sweeping descent to the village of Kingsand.

### Smugglers' Haven

Kingsand is a charming village, linked seamlessly by the long and narrow Garrett Street to the equally charming Cawsand. These were very successful smugglers' havens during the 18th and early 19th centuries. In Garrett Street, opposite the Halfway House Inn, look for a sign on the wall indicating the old Cornwall-Devon border. The Cornish side of Plymouth Sound was incorporated into Anglo-Saxon territory in 705 AD in order to secure both banks of the estuary against, mainly Viking, raids. Kingsand remained as part of Devon until 1844. From Kingsand the route follows the coastal footpath along the more bracing sea shore of Plymouth Sound. Finally you reach the delightful park environment that surrounds Mount Edgcumbe House where you can visit the house if you wish and explore the lovely gardens.

## Walk 4 **Directions**

① Go left along the footway opposite the car park entrance. Where the footway ends at an old fountain and horse trough, cross back left and go through a gap by a telephone kiosk, signposted 'Empacombe'. Keep left past the **Old School Rooms**. Turn right at a junction then pass an obelisk and follow the path alongside the tree-hidden creek to **Empacombe**.

② At a surfaced lane, by a house, keep ahead and go down to **Empacombe Quay**. Turn left beyond the low wall, (dogs under control please) and skirt the edge of the small harbour to reach a stone stile onto a wooded path. Continue round **Palmer Point** and on to a public road.

③ Go through the kissing gate opposite, signposted 'Maker Church, Kingsand'. Follow the track ahead for 55yds (50m), then bear right, up the open field (no obvious path) heading between telegraph poles, to find a faint path into Pigshill Wood. Bear right along a track, go left at signposts and climb uphill following footpath signs. Cross a track, then go up some stone steps to reach more steps onto a public road. Cross, with care, and follow a path to Maker Church.

---

**WHERE TO EAT AND DRINK** ℹ

Kingsand has a number of good pubs, restaurants and cafés. The Rising Sun is a pleasant, old style pub. It offers pasties, crab platter and local scallops. The Halfway House has some fine beers and does excellent meals with seafood a speciality. On the seafront is Cleave Tea Rooms, a licensed restaurant serving fresh crab. In Cremyll the Edgcumbe Arms is a traditional quayside inn with a pleasant terrace overlooking Plymouth Sound and offering a good selection of real ales and a varied menu. The Orangery Restaurant and Tea Room is located in the Old Orangery in Mount Edgcumbe estate's Italian garden.

---

④ Turn sharp right in front of the church, follow the field edge, then go over a stile on the left. Follow the next field edge and cross a stile on the left, then follow the path past a house and across a lane into a field. Cross two fields to a lane. Turn up right, then go left at a junction.

⑤ Where the road levels off, bear off left down a track at a public footpath signpost. Keep ahead at a

junction and, after a long level stretch, go left at a junction to reach Kingsand via Devonport Hill and Kingsway. To explore Kingsand and Cawsand, bear left down the narrow Heavitree Road.

⑥ To return to Cremyll, at Kingsway go through a gate into Mount Edgcumbe Country Park. Follow a good track to a public lane at Hooe Lake Valley.

⑦ Rejoin the coast path, signposted just a few paces along the lane. Keep to the upper path at a junction, then merge with another track from the left and continue through the woods.

⑧ A few paces after passing beneath an arch, bear off right from the main track and down a path zig-zagging steeply downhill to the coast. Follow the coast path back to Mount Edgcumbe and Cremyll.

---

**WHILE YOU'RE THERE** ℹ

Mount Edgcumbe House was built in the mid-16th century and subsequently enlarged. It was badly damaged by German incendiary bombs in 1941 and rebuilt in the 1960s. In 1971 house and estate were purchased jointly by Cornwall County Council and Plymouth City Council and the Mount Edgcumbe Country Park was established. The house is open to the public and has a fine collection of mainly modern furnishings and Victorian artefacts. There are paintings by artists such as Sir Joshua Reynolds. The surrounding gardens include the Earl's Garden, an 18th-century formal garden. The house is open, Wed–Sun and Bank Holiday Monday, from April to mid-October.

# The Busy Port of Dartmouth and a Spectacular Castle

*An easy round along the cliffs to Blackstone Point and Dartmouth Castle – and a ferry ride to the pub.*

| | |
|---|---|
| •DISTANCE• | 3 miles (4.8km) |
| •MINIMUM TIME• | 2hrs |
| •ASCENT / GRADIENT• | 115ft (35m) ▲▲▲ |
| •LEVEL OF DIFFICULTY• | 🚶 🚶 🚶 |
| •PATHS• | Easy coastal footpath and green lanes |
| •LANDSCAPE• | Farmland, cliff tops and river estuary |
| •SUGGESTED MAP• | aqua3 OS Outdoor Leisure 20 South Devon |
| •START / FINISH• | Grid reference: SX 874491 |
| •DOG FRIENDLINESS• | Possibility of livestock in some fields |
| •PARKING• | National Trust car parks at Little Dartmouth |
| •PUBLIC TOILETS• | Dartmouth Castle |

## BACKGROUND TO THE WALK

Dartmouth seems to have everything. The town has a rich and illustrious history and, with its smaller sister Kingswear on the opposite shore, occupies a commanding position on the banks of the Dart. With its sheltered, deep-water harbour it developed as a thriving port and shipbuilding town from the 12th century. By the 14th century it enjoyed a flourishing wine trade, and benefited from the profits of piracy for generations. Thomas Newcomen, who produced the first industrial steam engine, was born here in 1663. Today pleasure craft and the tourist industry have taken over in a big way – the annual Royal Regatta has been a major event for over 150 years – but Dartmouth has lost none of its charm. One of its attractions is that there are all sorts of ways of getting there: by bus, using the town's park-and-ride scheme, by river, on a steamer from Totnes, by sea, on a coastal trip from Torbay, by steam train, from Paignton or, of course, on foot along the coast path.

### Fortified River Mouth

Now cared for by English Heritage, 15th-century Dartmouth Castle enjoys an exceptionally beautiful position at the mouth of the Dart. Replacing the 1388 *fortalice* of John Hawley, it was one of the most advanced fortresses of the day and, with Kingswear Castle opposite (of which only the tower remains) was built to protect the homes and warehouses of the town's wealthy merchants. A chain was slung across the river mouth between the two fortifications, and guns fired from ports in the castle walls. Visitors can experience a representation of life in the later Victorian gun battery that was established. A record of 1192 infers that there was a monastic foundation on the site, leading to the establishment of St Petrock's Church, rebuilt in Gothic style within the castle precincts in 1641–2.

The cobbled quayside at Bayard's Cove, with its attractive and prosperous 17th- and 18th-century buildings (including the Customs House from 1739) was used during filming of the BBC TV series *The Onedin Line* in the 1970s. The wooded estuary a little upriver was also used for a scene supposedly set in 18th-century China, but filming was unwittingly

Walk 5

thwarted by the sound of a steam train chuffing through the trees! The single-storey artillery fort at Bayard's Cove was built before 1534 to protect the harbour. You can still see the gunports at ground level and the remains of a stairway leading to a walled walk above. A plaque commemorates the sailing of the *Mayflower* and *Speedwell* from the quay in 1620.

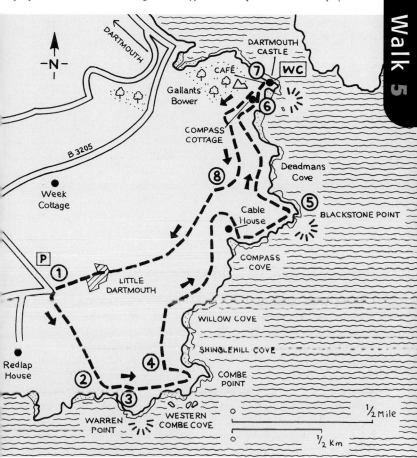

# Walk 5 Directions

① The car parks at **Little Dartmouth** are signposted off the B3205 (from the A379 Dartmouth-to-Stoke Fleming road). Go through the right-hand car park, following the signs 'Coast Path Dartmouth'. Continue through a kissing gate, keeping the hedge to your right. Walk through the next field, then through a kissing gate to join the coast path.

② Turn left; there are lovely views here west to **Start Point** and east towards the **Day Beacon** above **Kingswear**. The coast path runs a little inland from the cliff edge, but you can always go straight ahead to walk above **Warren Point** (a plaque reveals that the Devon Federation of Women's Institutes gave this land to the National Trust in 1970).

③ Continue left to pass above **Western Combe Cove** (with steps down to the sea) and then **Combe**

**Walk 5**

**Point** (take care – it's a long drop to the sea from here).

④ Rejoin the coast path through an open gateway in a wall and follow it above **Shinglehill Cove**. The path turns inland, passes through a gate, becomes narrow and a little overgrown, and twists along the back of **Willow Cove**. It passes through a wooded section (with a field on the left) and then climbs around the back of **Compass Cove**. Keep going to pass through a gate. Keep left to reach a wooden footpath post, then turn sharp right, down the valley to the cliff edge. Follow the path on, through a gate near **Blackstone Point**.

⑤ Leave the path right to clamber down onto the rocks here – you get a superb view over the mouth of the estuary. Retrace your steps and continue on the coast path as it turns inland along the side of the estuary and runs through deciduous woodland.

---

**WHAT TO LOOK FOR** ⓘ

**Dartmouth**, both on shore and on the water, is always buzzing with activity – it never stops. There's masses to watch including pleasure steamers, private cruisers, brightly-coloured dinghies, rowing boats, ferries, expensive ocean-going yachts, canoeists and even huge cruise ships, calling in for a night en route for sunnier climes. You'll also notice naval craft, ranging from old-fashioned whalers to modern frigates, and connected with the **Britannia Royal Naval College**, which overlooks the town. Princes Charles and Andrew both studied here. You may also hear the whistle of a steam train on the **Paignton-to-Kingswear railway**, which runs along the eastern side of the river to terminate at Kingswear Station.

---

**WHILE YOU'RE THERE** ⓘ

Catch the ferry from Stumpy Steps (just upriver from the castle), which within a few minutes will deposit you right in the centre of Dartmouth. You get a fabulous view of all those superb waterside residences that are tantalisingly difficult – if not impossible – to see from the lane above, and the ferry saves you a further mile (1.6km) walk. There's a continuous shuttle service from the castle from 10:15AM until 5PM.

---

⑥ The path meets a surfaced lane opposite **Compass Cottage**; go right onto the lane and immediately right again steeply downhill, keeping the wall to your left. At the turning space go right down steps to reach the castle and café.

⑦ Retrace your route up the steps to the tarmac lane at Point ⑥, then left to pass **Compass Cottage**, and straight on up the steep lane (signposted '**Little Dartmouth**') and through a kissing gate onto National Trust land.

⑧ The path runs along the top of a field and through a five-bar gate onto a green lane. Go through a gate and the farmyard at **Little Dartmouth** and ahead on a tarmac lane to the car park.

---

**WHERE TO EAT AND DRINK** ⓘ

There's the **Castle Tearooms** at Dartmouth Castle and, if you hop on the ferry, masses of very good eating places in Dartmouth – including the best takeaway prawn sandwiches ever, available from a shop on the right just past the lower ferry slipway. The **Royal Castle Hotel** overlooking the Boat Float in the middle of the town is a freehouse, with good food, as is the **Dartmouth Arms** at historic Bayard's Cove.

# The Birdlife of the Otter Estuary Nature Reserve

*Along the banks of the peaceful River Otter and the red sandstone cliffs towards High Peak.*

| | |
|---|---|
| **•DISTANCE•** | 4¼ miles (6.8km) |
| **•MINIMUM TIME•** | 2hrs |
| **•ASCENT / GRADIENT•** | 164ft (50m) ▲▲ ▲ ▲ |
| **•LEVEL OF DIFFICULTY•** | 🚶 🚶 🚶 |
| **•PATHS•** | Good level paths, coastal section and lanes, 2 stiles |
| **•LANDSCAPE•** | River meadow, cliffs and undulating farmland |
| **•SUGGESTED MAP•** | aqua3 OS Explorer 115 Exeter & Sidmouth |
| **•START / FINISH•** | Grid reference: SX 077830 |
| **•DOG FRIENDLINESS•** | Opportunities for dogs to run free; some livestock |
| **•PARKING•** | By side of broad, quiet lane near entrance to South Farm |
| **•PUBLIC TOILETS•** | None on main route. Try Otterton Mill |

## BACKGROUND TO THE WALK

Peaceful, tranquil, lush, idyllic these are all words that could easily be applied to this stroll along the banks of the River Otter. The river wends its way to meet the sea just east of Budleigh Salterton, its lower reaches a haven for a wealth of birdlife. In contrast to this, the walk continues along the top of the red sandstone cliffs typical of this area – but the coast path here is not in any way heart-thumpingly strenuous. The combination of the serene river meadows and the glorious coastal scenery – and then, perhaps, tea at Otterton Mill – make this an ideal family walk.

### The Otter Estuary Nature Reserve

The Nature Reserve, south of White Bridge and managed by the Devon Wildlife Trust, is one of the smallest in the South West. The estuary was much more extensive in the past, and 500 years ago cargo ships could travel upriver as far as Otterton. Today the estuary provides a haven for all kinds of birdlife, best seen between October and March. Oystercatchers, dunlins and other wading birds come to feed here; large flocks of waders and ducks, such as wigeons and teal, attract peregrine falcons, sparrowhawks and mink. There are over 200,000 wigeon on British estuaries, and it is one of our most common over-wintering species of duck. Three-quarters of the estuary has been colonised by saltmarsh, which is also home to warblers in the summer months, linnets and greenfinches all year round, and kingfishers in winter. To catch the action, about ¼ mile (400m) from the start of the main walk take a small path right towards the river to a birdwatching hide, run by the Devon Birdwatching and Preservation Society. Stop for a while and watch the activity on the waters below – there's always something happening.

The mid-section of the walk brings us within sight of Otterton, a large, pleasant village, with many traditional cob and thatch buildings. The church – St Michael and All Angels – is most impressive. There was a Saxon church here before the Norman Conquest, rebuilt by Benedictine monks when they established a priory in the 12th century. The main monastery building lay on the north side of the church, and part of it – probably the guests' hall – remains today. After Henry VIII's Dissolution of the Monasteries, in 1539, the church gradually fell into disrepair until it was, eventually, totally rebuilt in the 1870s. The design was by Benjamin Ferrey and the funding came from the Rt Hon Louisa Lady Rolle, a local dignitary. The church today is extremely grand and spacious, with superb blue marble columns along the nave. The west tower is built of the Old Red Sandstone we saw in the cliffs earlier in the walk.

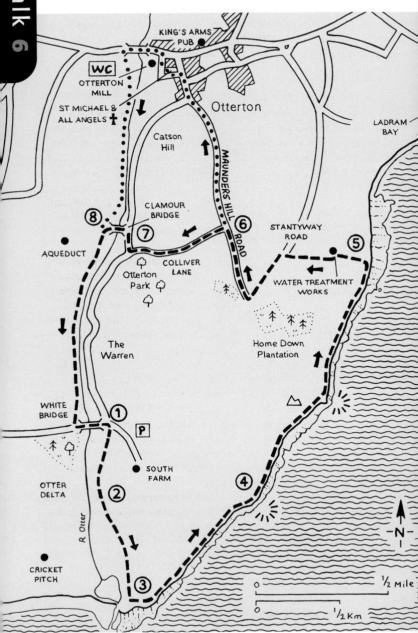

Walk 6

## Walk 6 **Directions**

① Walk through the kissing gate to the right of the gate to **South Farm**. Turn right following signs for 'Coast Path Ladram Bay'. The narrow, sandy path runs along the field edge, with lovely views right over the saltmarshes of the **Otter Estuary Nature Reserve** and the **River Otter**.

② At the end of that field a shallow flight of wooden steps leads to a walkway and footbridge, and up into the next field. There are good views downriver to the shingle bank at **Budleigh Salterton** and across the river to the cricket pitch.

> **WHILE YOU'RE THERE** ⓘ
> Visit **Bicton Park** and **Botanical Gardens**, straight over the B3178 from the road to Otterton. Bicton is open 364 days of the year, and has over 60 acres (24ha) of landscaped gardens, with a superb arboretum, lake and a secret garden, and a splendid 19th-century Palm House.

③ The path continues gently downhill until it turns sharply left following the line of the coast. Just before you turn east there are panoramic views right over the Otter delta, and along the beach.

④ After just over a mile (1.6km) the path rises a little, and you can see the whole of **Lyme Bay** ahead, including **High Peak** (564ft/157m one of the highest points on the South Devon coast). Follow the coast path: the red sandstone cliffs are extremely friable and 'chunks' continually tumble seawards, but the path is safe. Pass through a small gate by the ruined lookout building, and downhill.

⑤ Turn left to leave the coast path on the 'Permissive path to Otterton'; this narrow, grassy path leads over a stile; turn immediately left and follow the path right around the water treatment works, and up the gravelly lane to meet **Stantyway Road**. The lane veers right, but you should turn left up a grassy track, following signs to **Otterton** and the **River Otter**. The track soon veers right and gives way to a tarmac lane.

⑥ After 400yds (366m) **Colliver Lane** and the **River Otter** are signed to the left. Turn left here and follow a narrow, wooded green lane, which ends at a gate. Go through that, then almost immediately another, and follow the signs along the edge of the next field, which you leave over a stile onto a track.

⑦ Turn immediately left between two big ornamental brick pillars, and then right under a very large oak tree. Descend a short flight of steps and cross over the River **Otter** on **Clamour Bridge**, a wooden footbridge.

⑧ Turn left and follow the river south; over a small leat (look out for the aqueduct coming across the meadows on your right), through a gate and continue to **White Bridge**, where you go through a kissing gate, turn left and find your car.

> **WHERE TO EAT AND DRINK** ⓘ
> If you just do the main walk, drive up to the village of Otterton afterwards. The café at **Otterton Mill** is open daily from 10AM to 5PM (early closing in winter) and serves a great range of delicious wholefood dishes. The **King's Arms** (complete with its own post office) welcomes families, and has a beer garden and children's play area.

# Westhay Peatland Reserve

*A nature ramble through reconstructed peat marshland, including a brief walk on water.*

| | |
|---|---|
| •DISTANCE• | 4¾ miles (7.7km) |
| •MINIMUM TIME• | 2hrs 15min |
| •ASCENT / GRADIENT• | 250ft (80m) ▲ ▲ ▲ |
| •LEVEL OF DIFFICULTY• | 🚶 🚶 🚶 |
| •PATHS• | Mostly smooth, level paths and tracks, 2 stiles |
| •LANDSCAPE• | Reed beds and water-meadows |
| •SUGGESTED MAP• | aqua3 OS Explorer 141 Cheddar Gorge |
| •START / FINISH• | Grid reference: ST 456437 |
| •DOG FRIENDLINESS• | On leads in reserve, can be free on drove tracks |
| •PARKING• | Free car park at Decoy Pool, signposted from public road |
| •PUBLIC TOILETS• | None on route |
| •NOTE• | To bypass rough part, follow lane between Points ④ and ⑥ |

## BACKGROUND TO THE WALK

At Westhay Moor the Somerset Trust for Nature Conservation (STNC) is carefully recreating the original peat wetland from a time before drainage and peat cuttings. This involves raising the water table with polythene barriers, and importing sphagnum moss and peatland plants from Cumbria. 'True blanket bog', one of their notices reminds us, 'should wobble when walked on...' And while these rehabilitated peat diggings are very good news for waterfowl and the nightjar, for rare spiders and the bog bush cricket, they are still a long way from the original Somerset moor.

### Moor or Morass?

'Moor' is the same as 'mire' or 'morass'; the Saxon word first occurs in the account of King Alfred taking refuge at Muchelney. For the Saxons the moor was a place of mystery and fear. About 1,500 years ago the monster Grendel was the original 'Thing from the Swamp' in the poem of *Beowulf*. Open water alternated with reed beds and mud. The inhabitants moved around by boat, or by wading, or on stilts. Even if you could see out over the reeds it rarely helped as the mist would come down. And, at nightfall, the will o' the wisp misled you into the unstable mud, just in case you hadn't been swallowed up in it already.

If you did ever get out on to firm land, you were quite likely to be infected with ague or marsh fever. Even the modern name, 'malaria', reflects its supposed origin in the misty airs of the wetlands. Actually it was transmitted by mosquitoes that bred in the stagnant water. Oliver Cromwell, a fenman from East Anglia, died of malaria. It persisted in the marshes of Essex into the 20th century and may return with global warming in the 21st.

### Wet Refuge

For those who knew its ways, the moor was the safest of refuges. Iron Age tribes built a village on wooden piles near Glastonbury; the Romans complained of the way the tribesmen would hide with only their heads above the water. Alfred found safety from the Danes here, as did the monks of Glastonbury.

### Wealth in the Wet

The moor was also, in its own way, wealthy. The less wet sections grew a rich summer pasture, fertilised by the silt of the winter floods. It's no coincidence that Britain's most famous cheese comes from the edge of the Levels. The deep, moist soil also grew heavy crops of hemp. Henry VIII made the growing of this useful plant compulsory, as it supplied cordage and sailcloth for the navy. Today, under its Latin name of *Cannabis sativa*, it is, of course, strictly forbidden. The wetter ground yielded osiers for baskets and reed for thatch; wildfowl and fish; and goosefeather quills for penmen. Fuel was peat, or willow poles from the pollarded trees whose roots supported the ditches. And the rent for this desirable property was often paid in live eels.

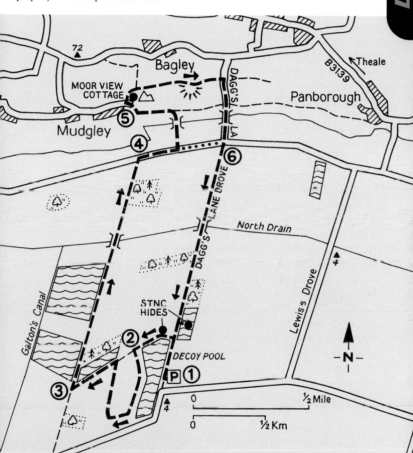

## Walk 7 **Directions**

① Head into the reserve on a broad track, with **Decoy Pool** hiding behind reeds on the left. At the end of the lake a kissing gate leads to the STNC hide, with a broad path

continuing between high reedbeds. Ignore a gate on the left ('No Visitor Access') but go through a kissing gate 60yds (55m) further on.

② A fenced track runs through peat ground, where birches are being felled to recreate blanket bog.

**Walk 7**

The track turns right; now take a kissing gate on the left for a path through trees. At its end a new track leads back through the peat. At the end turn left to reach a gate on to the next of the 'droves' or raised trackways through the peatland.

③ Turn right, passing hides and crossing a bridge over the wide **North Drain**; the land on each side now comprises water-meadows. The track leads to a lane.

④ If you wish to omit the field paths above (which are rough, but give a splendid view over the reserve), simply turn right, going along the road for 650yds (594m) to a junction, Point ⑥. Otherwise turn right as far as a right-hand bend, and continue for 175yds (160m) to where gates are on both sides of the road. Go through the left-hand one (with a red-painted marker) and cross to a gate and bridge over a ditch. Follow the left edge of the next field to its corner. Turn left through a gate and follow field edges to a small orchard. Turn right, up to the end of a tarred lane.

⑤ Turn left along the road to an uphill path to the left of **Moor View Cottage** – this becomes overgrown and quite steep – to a stile on the right. Cross the tops of five fields. In the sixth field drop slightly to pass below farm buildings (there is a helpful signpost here). A gate leads into a small orchard, with a signposted gate on to **Dagg's Lane** just above. Turn down the lane to the road below.

⑥ Directly opposite Dagg's Lane is the track, **Dagg's Lane Drove**. This runs between meadows then re-enters the reserve, passing between pools left by peat extraction. Look out for a path on the left signposted to a hide. This leads out excitingly on stilts above the flooded mire. Return from the hide and rejoin the drove track, which quickly leads back to the car park.

# Lulworth to Durdle Door

*An exhilarating walk on a spectacular piece of coastline.*

| | |
|---|---|
| •DISTANCE• | 6¾ miles (10.9km) |
| •MINIMUM TIME• | 3hrs 30min |
| •ASCENT / GRADIENT• | 1,247ft (380m) ▲▲▲ |
| •LEVEL OF DIFFICULTY• | 🚶 🚶 🚶 |
| •PATHS• | Stone path, grassy tracks, tarmac, muddy field path, 8 stiles |
| •LANDSCAPE• | Steeply rolling cliffs beside sea, green inland |
| •SUGGESTED MAP• | aqua3 OS Explorer OL 15 Purbeck & South Dorset |
| •START / FINISH• | Grid reference: SY 821800 |
| •DOG FRIENDLINESS• | Excitable dogs need strict control near cliff edge |
| •PARKING• | Pay-and-display car park (busy), signed at Lulworth Cove |
| •PUBLIC TOILETS• | Beside Heritage Centre; also just above Lulworth Cove |

## BACKGROUND TO THE WALK

Lulworth Cove is an almost perfectly circular bay in the rolling line of cliffs that form Dorset's southern coast. Its pristine condition and geological importance earned it World Heritage status in 2002. The cove provides a secure anchorage for small fishing boats and pleasure craft, and a sun trap of safe water for summer bathers. The cliffs around the eastern side of the bay are crumbly soft and brightly coloured in some places, while around the opposite arm the rock appears to have been folded and shoved aside by an unseen hand. The geology is intriguing and a visit to the Heritage Centre will help you to sort it out.

The oldest layer, easily identified here, is the gleaming white Portland stone. This attractive stone was much employed by Christopher Wren in his rebuilding of London. It is a fine-grained oolite, around 140 million years old. It consists of tightly compressed, fossilised shells – the flat-coiled ones are ammonites. Occasional giant ammonites, called titanites, may be seen incorporated into house walls across Purbeck. Like the rock of Bat's Head, it may contain speckled bands of flinty chert. Above this is a layer of Purbeck marble, a limestone rich in the fossils of vertebrates. This is where dinosaur, fish and reptile fossils are usually found. The soft layer above this consists of Wealden beds, a belt of colourful clays, silts and sands, that are unstable and prone to landslips when exposed.

Crumbly, white chalk overlays the Wealden beds. The chalk consists of the remains of microscopic sea creatures and shells deposited over a long period of time when a deep sea covered much of Dorset, some 75 million years ago. This is the chalk that underlies Dorset's famous downland and is seen in the exposed soft, eroded cliffs at White Nothe. Hard nodules and bands of flint appear in the chalk – it's a purer type of chert – and in its gravel beach form it protects long stretches of this fragile coast.

The laying down of chalk marks the end of the Cretaceous period in geology. After this the blanket of chalk was uplifted, folded and subjected to erosion by the slow, inexorable movement of tectonic plates. The Dorset coast was exposed to some of its most extreme pressure between 24 and 1½ million years ago, resulting in folding, crumpling and sometimes overturning of strata. You can see this in the vertical strata on rocks around Durdle Door and Stair Hole.

Walk 8

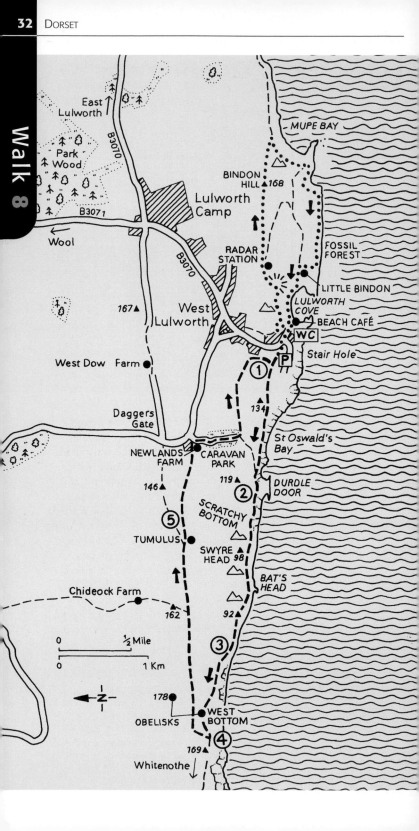

East Lulworth

Park Wood

B3070

B3071

Wool

Lulworth Camp

MUPE BAY

BINDON HILL ▲168

RADAR STATION

FOSSIL FOREST

LITTLE BINDON

LULWORTH COVE

BEACH CAFÉ

WC

167▲

West Lulworth

West Dow Farm

P

Stair Hole

①

134▲

St Oswald's Bay

Daggers Gate

NEWLANDS FARM

CARAVAN PARK

119▲

②

DURDLE DOOR

146▲

⑤

SCRATCHY BOTTOM

TUMULUS

SWYRE HEAD ▲98

BAT'S HEAD

Chideock Farm

162▲

92▲

③

0       ½ Mile

0       1 Km

←N→

178▲

OBELISKS

WEST BOTTOM

169▲

④

Whitenothe

**Walk 8 Directions**

① Find a stile at the back of the car park. Cross this to take the broad, paved footpath that leads up some shallow steps to the top of the first hill. Continue along the brow, and down the other side. Pass below a **caravan park** and cross a stile.

② Reach the cove of **Durdle Door**, almost enclosed from the sea by a line of rocks. A flight of steps leads down to the sea here, but carry on walking straight ahead on the coast path and the natural stone arch of the Door itself is revealed in a second cove below you. The mass of Swyre Head looms close and yes, that is the path you're going to take, ascending straight up the side. Walk down to the bottom then climb back up to **Swyre Head**. The path leads steeply down again on the other side, to a short stretch overlooking **Bat's Head**. Climb the next steep hill. Continue along the path behind the cliffs, where the land tilts away from the sea.

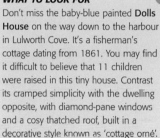

**WHERE TO EAT AND DRINK**
In Lulworth the **Heritage Centre café** includes family meals and baguettes. Just down the hill, the **Lulworth Cove Hotel** is open all year and serves a multitude of fresh, locally caught fish.

③ The path climbs more gently up the next hill. Pass a **navigation obelisk** on the right, and follow the path as it curves round the contour above **West Bottom**.

④ At a marker stone that indicates Whitenothe ahead turn right, over a stile, and follow a fence inland. The path curves round so you're walking parallel with the coast on level greensward. Pass three stone embrasures with shell sculptures inside, and a second obelisk. Go through a gate. Now keep straight ahead along the top of the field and across a crossing of paths, signed to Daggers Gate. Go through a gateway and straight on. The path starts to descend gently. In the next field the path becomes more of a track. Bear right to pass close by a tumulus and reach a stile.

**WHAT TO LOOK FOR**
Don't miss the baby-blue painted **Dolls House** on the way down to the harbour in Lulworth Cove. It's a fisherman's cottage dating from 1861. You may find it difficult to believe that 11 children were raised in this tiny house. Contrast its cramped simplicity with the dwelling opposite, with diamond-pane windows and a cosy thatched roof, built in a decorative style known as 'cottage orné'.

⑤ Cross this and walk along the top of the field, above **Scratchy Bottom**. Cross a stile into a green lane leading to **Newlands Farm**. Follow it round to the right, and turn right into the caravan park. Go straight ahead on the road through here. At the far side cross a stile and turn left, signed to West Lulworth. Stay along the field edge, cross a stile and walk above a farm lane, around the end of the hill. Keep straight on at the fingerpost and reach the stiles above the car park. Turn left and retrace your route.

**WHILE YOU'RE THERE**
At nearby East Lulworth is **Lulworth Castle Park**. The castle itself, a 17th-century hunting lodge built four-square with pepperpot towers, is a handsome shell, but was gutted by fire in 1929 and only partly restored. Other attractions on the estate include a circular chapel, an animal farm and an adventure playground for children.

**Walk 8**

# Great Bedwyn and the Kennet and Avon Canal

*Combine a peaceful walk beside the Kennet and Avon Canal with a visit to Wiltshire's only working windmill and the beam engines at Crofton.*

| | |
|---|---|
| •DISTANCE• | 5½ miles (8.8km) |
| •MINIMUM TIME• | 2hrs |
| •ASCENT / GRADIENT• | 147ft (45m) ▲ ▲▲ |
| •LEVEL OF DIFFICULTY• | 🚶🚶 🚶🚶 🚶🚶 |
| •PATHS• | Field paths, woodland tracks, tow path, roads, 1 stile |
| •LANDSCAPE• | Farmland, woodland, canal and village scenery |
| •SUGGESTED MAP• | aqua3 OS Explorer 157 Marlborough & Savernake Forest |
| •START / FINISH• | Grid reference: SU 279645 |
| •DOG FRIENDLINESS• | Dogs can be off lead along tow path |
| •PARKING• | Great Bedwyn Station |
| •PUBLIC TOILETS• | Crofton Pumping Station, portaloo at Wilton Windmill |

## BACKGROUND TO THE WALK

Situated beside a peaceful stretch of the Kennet and Avon Canal, the large village of Great Bedwyn was formerly a market town, with borough status from the 11th century until the Reform Act of 1832, it even returned two Members of Parliament. It still has the appearance of a small town with a wide main street, continuous rows of cottages, a few elegant town houses and the flint Church of St Mary the Virgin, one of the largest and finest churches in the area, set in low lying land close to the canal.

### Kennet and Avon Canal

Undeniably, the main reason most visitors come to Great Bedwyn is to enjoy the sights and sounds of the Kennet and Avon Canal and the beautiful scenery it meanders through south west of the village. It was in 1788 that the idea of linking the River Kennet, which flows into the Thames at Reading, with the River Avon at Bath by means of an artificial waterway was first mooted. The navigation between the rivers had to rise to 450ft (137m) and then descend on the other side and needed 104 locks, two aqueducts and, at the summit, a tunnel over 500yds (457m) long. Construction on the ambitious project, designed by John Rennie (1761–1821), started in 1794 and was completed in 1810. The canal was used to carry vast quantities of coal from the Somerset coalfield, iron, stone and slate, local agricultural products and timber, and to bring luxuries like tobacco and spirits from London to Bath, Bristol and the intervening towns.

### Decline and Restoration

Transporting goods along the canal proved successful for 40 years then, with the completion of the railways offering faster and more efficient transport, the canal began to fall into decline. Since 1962 the Kennet and Avon Canal Trust and British Waterways have revitalised the navigable waterway by clearing the waters and locks for leisure barges and making the banks and tow paths accessible to anglers, naturalists and walkers.

Also part of the restoration scheme, and the highlight of your walk along the tow path, are the magnificent beam engines at Crofton Pumping Station. The two beam engines, the 1812 Boulton and Watt and the 1845 Harvey of Hale, operate a huge cast-iron beam and were used to raise water from Wilton Water to the summit level of the canal. Beautifully restored and powered by steam from a hand-stoked, coal-fired Lancashire boiler, you may be lucky to see them working if you're visiting on a summer weekend.

## Wilton Windmill

The county's only complete surviving working windmill stands proudly on a chalk hilltop overlooking the canal. Built in 1821, after the construction of the canal had diverted the water previously used to power mills, it is a five-storey brick tower mill and was fully operational until the 1890s. It closed and became derelict in the 1920s. Restored in the 1970s and floodlit at night, you can once again see local corn being ground into flour.

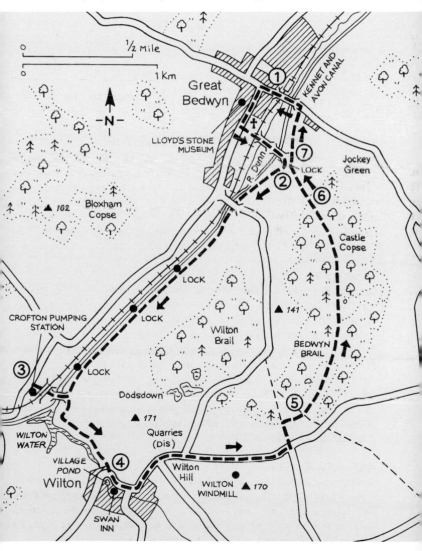

Walk 9

# Walk 9 Directions

① Walk back to the main road in Great Bedwyn and turn right, then left down **Church Street**. Pass **Lloyd's Stone Museum** and the church, then take the footpath left between the two graveyards. Climb a stile, cross a field to a kissing gate, then carefully cross the railway line to a further kissing gate. Cross the footbridge, then the bridge over the **Kennet and Avon Canal** and descend to the tow path.

**WHAT TO LOOK FOR** ℹ
In **St Mary's Church**, Great Bedwyn, look for the tomb of Sir John Seymour in the chancel. His daughter Jane was Henry VIII's third and best loved wife.

② Turn right, pass beneath the bridge and continue along the tow path for 1½ miles (2.4km), passing three locks, to reach **Lock 60**. Cross the canal here, turn left, then follow a wooded path right and pass through the tunnel beneath the railway. Ascend steps to the **Crofton Pumping Station**.

③ Retrace your steps back to the tow path and Lock 60. Take the footpath right, waymarked to Wilton Windmill, and walk beside **Wilton Water** along the edge of fields. Eventually, turn right down a short track to a lane by the village pond in **Wilton**.

**WHERE TO EAT AND DRINK** ℹ
Great Bedwyn has two pubs, the **Cross Keys** and the **Three Tuns**, and a bakery. Light refreshments are available if visiting the **Crofton Beam Engines**, while at Wilton, the homely **Swan Inn** offers decent doorstop sandwiches, home-cooked pub dishes, good Sunday lunches and a selection of real ales.

④ Turn left, then just past the **Swan Inn**, follow the lane left, signed 'Great Bedwyn'. Climb out of the village and fork right to pass **Wilton Windmill**. Continue along the lane and turn left on to a track, opposite the lane to Marten. Just before the wooded track snakes downhill, turn right along a bridle path (unsigned) beside woodland.

⑤ At a staggered crossing of paths, turn right, then in 50yds (46m), turn left, signed 'Great Bedwyn'. Proceed down a well-surfaced track and go through a gate into **Bedwyn Brail**. Continue though the woods, following signs to Great Bedwyn. Go straight across a clearing before forking left to re-enter the woods in the left-hand corner of the clearing.

⑥ On emerging in a field corner, keep left along the field boundary, go through a gap in the hedge and descend along the left-hand side of the next field, with **Great Bedwyn** visible ahead. Near the bottom of the field, bear half-right, downhill to the canal.

⑦ Pass through a gate by a bridge and **Lock 64** and turn right along the tow path. Go through the car park to the road, then turn left over the canal and rail bridges before turning right back to **Great Bedwyn Station**.

**WHILE YOU'RE THERE** ℹ
Visit **Lloyd's Stone Museum** in Great Bedwyn, a fascinating little open-air museum that demonstrates the art of stonemasonry. Here you can see monuments, gravestones and sculpture dating back to the 18th century. Just north of Great Bedwyn is **Chisbury Camp**, an ancient hill fort with the ruins of a 13th-century chapel standing within its 50ft (15m) high earth ramparts.

# Tennyson's Freshwater

*From lofty downland with magnificent coastal views to tranquil estuary scenes, this exhilarating ramble explores the landscape the poet loved so well.*

| | |
|---|---|
| •DISTANCE• | 6 miles (9.7km) |
| •MINIMUM TIME• | 3hrs |
| •ASCENT / GRADIENT• | 623ft (190m) ▲ ▲ ▲ |
| •LEVEL OF DIFFICULTY• | 🚶 🚶 🚶 |
| •PATHS• | Downland, field and woodland paths, some road walking and stretch of disused railway, 4 stiles |
| •LANDSCAPE• | Downland, farmland, freshwater marsh and salt marsh |
| •SUGGESTED MAP• | aqua3 OS Outdoor Leisure 29 Isle of Wight |
| •START / FINISH• | Grid reference: SZ 346857 |
| •DOG FRIENDLINESS• | Let off lead on Tennyson Down and along old railway |
| •PARKING• | Pay-and-display car park at Freshwater Bay |
| •PUBLIC TOILETS• | Freshwater Bay and Yarmouth |

## BACKGROUND TO THE WALK

Away from the hustle and bustle of the traditional resort towns, West Wight is a quieter, less populated area of great natural beauty, offering areas of open countryside, rugged cliffs, wonderful views and a fascinating wildlife. This exhilarating ramble encapsulates the contrasting landscapes of the area, from the wildlife rich tidal estuary of the River Yar and the natural wetland habitat of freshwater marshes, to rolling farmland and the magnificent chalk headlands and hills with their breathtaking coastal views.

### Solitary Walks

Of the many literary greats who sought seclusion and inspiration on the Island during the 19th century, it was the poet Alfred, Lord Tennyson who chose to reside in West Wight. Tennyson and his wife Emily first came to Farringford House, a castellated late-Georgian house (now a hotel) set in parkland beneath Tennyson Down, in 1853. From the drawing room he could look out across Freshwater Bay and the slopes of Afton Down, a view he believed to be the most beautiful in England – 'Mediterranean in its richness and charm'. Almost daily he would take long solitary walks across the chalk downland, enjoying the bracing air, which he declared to be 'worth sixpence a pint'. The island inspired some of his greatest poems. *The Charge of the Light Brigade* was written on the Down that now bears his name, and *Maud*, *Enoch Arden* and the *Idylls of the King* were all written at Farringford.

Tennyson's poetry was so popular that he soon became one of the richest poets in the country. Combined with his magnetic genius and personality, he soon changed the face of West Wight, as tiny Freshwater became the cultural centre of England, attracting the most eminent Victorians of his age – Charles Kingsley, Garibaldi, Lewis Carroll, Charles Darwin, Prince Albert – to name but a few. Farringford was the perfect place to entertain friends and celebrities, despite or because of its remoteness, but it was his time spent alone wandering the Downs or with his wife Emily in their fine garden that made Farringford so special. They bought a house on the mainland and only returned to Farringford for the winter, when they would be undisturbed. Alfred died in 1892 and Emily nearly four years later in 1896.

Memories of the great man and his family are dotted along this walk. On Tennyson Down, where he often rambled, you will find the granite monument erected in his honour in 1897. On quieter days you can imagine the poet striding up the hill, dressed in his flowing Spanish cloak, wide-brimmed hat and with a stout holly stick, for his favourite downland walk. You can take lunch or afternoon tea at Farringford Hotel. In Freshwater, step inside All Saints Church to view the memorials to the family, while in the peaceful churchyard you will find Emily's grave and a lovely view across the serene estuary of the River Yar.

**Walk 10** Wialk 10

# Walk 10 Directions

① From the car park, turn right along the road, then left before the bus shelter along a metalled track, signed '**Coastal Footpath**'. As it bears left, keep ahead through kissing gates and soon begin a steep ascent up a concrete path on to **Tennyson Down**. Keep to the well walked path to the memorial cross at its summit.

② Continue down the wide grassy swathe, which narrows between gorse bushes, to reach the replica of the **Old Nodes Beacon**. Here, turn very sharp right down a chalk track. At a junction (car park right) keep straight on up the narrow path.

> **WHILE YOU'RE THERE** ⓘ
> Visit the **Needles Pleasure Park** at Alum Bay. Take the spectacular chairlift to the beach to view the strange multi-coloured sands for which it is famous, take a boat trip to view the Needles at close quarters, and explore the restored Old Battery, built in 1862, with its viewing platform and exhibition of the history of the headland.

③ The path widens, then descends to a gate into woodland. Proceed close to the woodland fringe to a further gate and enter more open countryside. Pass disused excavations on the right, then shortly, turn sharp left down an unmarked path. Cross a stile, then keep left along the field boundary and bear sharp left to a stile. Cross the next field to a stile and turn right along the field edge to a stile.

④ Cross a farm track, go through a gate and walk along the track (F47) beside **Farringford Manor Hotel**. Pass beneath a wooden footbridge

and continue downhill to a gate and the road. (Turn left if wishing to visit the hotel). Turn right, pass the thatched church and turn left down **Blackbridge Road**. Just before **Black Bridge**, turn left into **Afton Marshes Nature Reserve**.

⑤ Join the nature trail, following the left-hand path beside the stream to the A3055 (this can be very wet in winter). Turn left and almost immediately cross over to join footpath F61 along the course of the old railway. In ½ mile (800m) reach the **Causeway**. Turn left here to visit **Freshwater church** and the **Red Lion**.

⑥ Turn right and follow the lane to the B3399. Turn left and shortly cross into unmetalled **Manor Road**. In a few paces, bear off left, signed '**Freshwater Way**', and ascend across grassland towards **Afton Down**.

⑦ Proceed ahead at a junction of paths beside the golf course, soon to follow the gravel track right to the clubhouse. Go through a gate, pass in front of the building and walk down the access track, keeping left to the A3055. Turn right downhill into **Freshwater Bay**.

> **WHAT TO LOOK FOR** ⓘ
> As you walk through the reedbeds and scrub of **Afton Marsh Nature Reserve**, look out for the blue flash of the kingfisher and the yellow blooms of the marsh marigold, among many other birds and marsh plants that thrive there. On Tennyson Down you may see rare chalk-loving flowers and grasses, including bee orchids and nettle-leaved bellflowers, and hundred of small butterflies, such as common, chalkhill, small and Adonis blues, skippers and dark green fritillaries.

**Walk 11**

# Bursledon and Boatbuilding

*Exploring both sides of the yacht-filled Hamble estuary.*

| | |
|---|---|
| •DISTANCE• | 6 miles (9.7km) |
| •MINIMUM TIME• | 3hrs |
| •ASCENT / GRADIENT• | 164ft (50m) ▲ ▲ ▲ |
| •LEVEL OF DIFFICULTY• | 🚶🚶 🚶🚶 🚶🚶 |
| •PATHS• | Riverside, field and woodland paths, some stretches of road |
| •LANDSCAPE• | River estuary, farmland dotted with patches of woodland |
| •SUGGESTED MAP• | aqua3 OS Outdoor Leisure 22 New Forest |
| •START / FINISH• | Grid reference: SU 485067 |
| •DOG FRIENDLINESS• | Keep dogs on lead |
| •PARKING• | Pay-and-display car park by Quay in Hamble |
| •PUBLIC TOILETS• | Hamble |

## BACKGROUND TO THE WALK

The tidal Hamble estuary between Bursledon and the Southampton Water is not only one of the longest in the county, it's also one of Britain's busiest. The river has a long history of human activity from the first Saxon settlers, who used it as a route to the fertile areas inland, to its current status as Britain's premier yachting centre. Today, this stretch of river is filled with yachts and pleasure craft, but between the 14th and the early 19th century both Hamble-le-Rice (its formal name) and Bursledon were major centres for naval shipbuilding.

### Great Shipbuilders

The valley provided a rich supply of timber for the wooden warships, the ironworks at nearby Hungerford Bottom supplied essential fastenings and the bend in the river at Bursledon offered the necessary shelter for the Hamble to be ideal for this vital industry. At its peak during the Napoleonic Wars the Elephant Yard, next to the Jolly Sailor pub, built the 74-gun HMS *Elephant*, Nelson's flagship at the Battle of Copenhagen. Two great local shipbuilders were George Parsons, who built the *Elephant*, and Philemon Ewer, who died in 1750 and whose epitaph states 'during the late war with France and Spain built seven large ships of war'. The best known ship to be built at Hamble was the *Grace Dieu* for Henry V in the 15th century. It was at Hamble Common in 1545 that Henry VIII watched in horror as his famous flagship, the 91-gun *Mary Rose*, sank with the loss of 700 men just off the coast.

The six tiny Victory Cottages you pass in Lower Swanwick, just a stone's throw from the present-day Moody's yard, were built in the late 18th century to house shipyard workers during the Napoleonic Wars. The bustling marinas and yacht moorings at Bursledon, best viewed from the terrace of the Jolly Sailor, have only appeared in the last 70 years.

Today, the villages of Hamble and Old Bursledon are a delight to explore. Hamble has a twisting main street, lined with pretty Georgian buildings, leading down to the Quay with lovely river views. Old Bursledon has a High Street but no shops, just peaceful lanes dotted with interesting buildings, in particular the timber-framed Dolphin, a former pub, with a 16th-century porch. Tucked away on the slopes above the river and scattered along lanes leading nowhere, you'll find it a pleasure to stroll through, especially if you pause at the Hacketts Marsh viewpoint where a well-placed bench affords the chance to admire the view.

Windmill

Manor Farm
Country Park

Bursledon
Hall

A 27

M 27

A 3025

B 3397

Bursledon

BURSLEDON
BRIDGE

THE
JOLLY SAILOR

BURSLEDON
BRICKWORKS

MARINA

③

MOODY'S
BOATYARD

⑤

TELEPHONE
BOX

④

VICTORY
COTTAGES

MALLARDS
MOOR

HACKETTS
MARSH

SALTERS
LANE

Sewage
Works

Brooklands
Farm

Sarisbury

⑥

②  BOATYARD

MARINA

Holly Hill
Woodland
Park

Airfield
disused )

Hamble
-le-Rice

MARINA

Hamble

Cawte's
Copse

⑦

Warsash

MARINA

Bunny
Meadows

P

①

WC

PASSENGER
FERRY

½ Mile

1 Km

-N-

## Walk 11 Directions

① From the quayside car park, walk to the pontoon and take the passenger ferry across the estuary to **Warsash** (weather permitting Monday–Friday 7AM–5PM; Saturday, Sunday 9AM–6PM). Turn left along the raised gravel path beside the estuary and mudflats. Cross a footbridge and continue to a gravelled parking area. During exceptionally high tides the path may flood, so walk through the car park and rejoin it by the marina.

---

### WHERE TO EAT AND DRINK ℹ

There's a range of pubs and tea rooms in Hamble, notably the **Compass Point Café**, **Village Tea Rooms** and the **Bugle**. Stop off at the **Jolly Sailor** in Bursledon for good ale and fine river views, or the quieter **Vine** in Old Bursledon.

---

② At a boatyard, keep right of a boat shed. Bear left beyond, between the shed and **TS Marina**, and bear right in front of the **Sales Office** to rejoin the path. Reach a lane, turn left and pass **Victory Cottages** on your right. Continue by **Moody's Boatyard** to the A27.

③ Turn left and cross **Bursledon Bridge**. (Turn right before the bridge to visit **Bursledon Brickworks**). Pass beneath the railway and turn left, signed to 'the Station'. Turn left into **Station Road**, then left again into the station car park, following signs for

---

### WHAT TO LOOK FOR ℹ

Just before high tide you may see up to 12 species of **waders**, including dunlin, redshank, lapwing and curlew, and wildfowl – shelduck, teal and Brent geese (in winter) – feeding on the rich mudflats as you stroll the riverside path.

---

the **Jolly Sailor**. Climb a steep path to the road. Turn left at the junction, then left again to reach the pub.

④ Return along the lane and fork left along the **High Street** into **Old Bursledon**. Pause at the excellent viewpoint at **Hacketts Marsh**, then bear left at the telephone box along the **High Street**. Pass the **Vine Inn** and **Salterns Lane**, then at a right bend, bear off left by **Thatched Cottage** along a footpath.

⑤ Join a metalled lane beside the drive to the **Coach House** then, as the lane curves left, keep ahead beside a house called **Woodlands**, following the path downhill to a stream. Proceed uphill through woodland (**Mallards Moor**). At a junction of paths on the woodland fringe, bear left with the bridleway, then at a concrete road bear right, then left to join a fenced path.

---

### WHILE YOU'RE THERE ℹ

Visit **Bursledon Brickworks**. Restored by a trust in 1990, it is the last surviving example of a steam-driven brickworks in the country, with a working steam engine, exhibition on the history and development of brickmaking, hands-on activities and special events.

---

⑥ Cross a railway bridge and soon pass a barrier to a road. Keep left round a sharp left-hand bend. Look out for a waymarked footpath on your right and follow this path behind houses for ½ mile (800m).

⑦ Join a metalled path and proceed past modern housing to a road. Follow this out to **Hamble Lane** and turn left to join the **High Street**. At the roundabout, bear right down **Lower High Street** back to the **Quay** and car park.

# West Itchenor – Harbour Sails and Trails

*Chichester Harbour's plentiful wildlife and colourful yachting activity form the backdrop to this fascinating waterside walk.*

**Walk 12**

| | |
|---|---|
| •DISTANCE• | 3½ miles (5.7km) |
| •MINIMUM TIME• | 1hr 30min |
| •ASCENT / GRADIENT• | Negligible ▲ ▲ ▲ |
| •LEVEL OF DIFFICULTY• | 🚶 🚶 🚶 |
| •PATHS• | Shoreline, field tracks and paths, 1 stile |
| •LANDSCAPE• | Open farmland and coastal scenery |
| •SUGGESTED MAP• | aqua3 OS Explorer 120 Chichester, South Harting & Selsey |
| •START / FINISH• | Grid reference: SZ 797013 |
| •DOG FRIENDLINESS• | Waterside paths are ideal for dogs but keep under control on stretches of open farmland and on short section of road. Dogs permitted on harbour water tour |
| •PARKING• | Large pay-and-display car park in West Itchenor |
| •PUBLIC TOILETS• | West Itchenor |

## BACKGROUND TO THE WALK

Weekend sailors flock to Chichester's vast natural harbour, making it one of the most popular attractions on the south coast. The harbour has about 50 miles (81km) of shoreline and 17 miles (28km) of navigable channel, though there is almost no commercial traffic. The Romans cast an approving eye over this impressive stretch of water and established a military base and harbour at nearby Fishbourne after the Claudian invasion of Britain in AD 43. Charles II had a fondness for the area too and kept a yacht here.

### Boat Building Legacy

Situated at the confluence of the Bosham and Chichester channels of the estuary is the sailing village of Itchenor, with its main street of picturesque houses and cottages running down to the waterfront. Originally named Icenor, this small settlement started life as a remote, sparsely populated community, but by the 18th century it had begun to play a vital role in the shipbuilding industry. Small warships were built here by the merchants of Chichester, though in later years shipbuilding ceased altogether and any trace of its previous prosperity disappeared beneath the houses and the harbour mud. However, the modern age of leisure and recreation has seen a revival in boat building and yachting and today Itchenor is once again bustling with boat yards, sailors and chandlers.

### Important Tidal Habitat

But there is much more to Chichester Harbour than sailing. Take a stroll along the harbour edge and you will find there is much to capture the attention. With its inter-tidal habitats, the harbour is a haven for plant life and wildlife. Wading birds such as curlew, redshank and dunlin can be seen using their differently shaped bills to extract food from the ecologically rich mudflats and terns may be spotted plunging to catch fish. Plants include sea lavender and glasswort and many of them are able to resist flooding and changing saltiness. Salt marsh is one of the typical habitats of Chichester Harbour and the plants which make up the marsh grow in different places according to how often they are flooded.

Stand on the hard at West Itchenor and you can look across the water towards neighbouring Bosham, pronounced 'Bozzum'. Better still, take the ferry over there and explore the delights of this picturesque harbour village. It was from here that Harold left for Normandy before the Norman Conquest of 1066. 'The sea creek, the green field, the grey church,' wrote Tennyson and this sums up perfectly the charm of this unspoilt corner of Sussex. Take a little time to have a look at the Church of the Holy Trinity and its Saxon tower base while you're there.

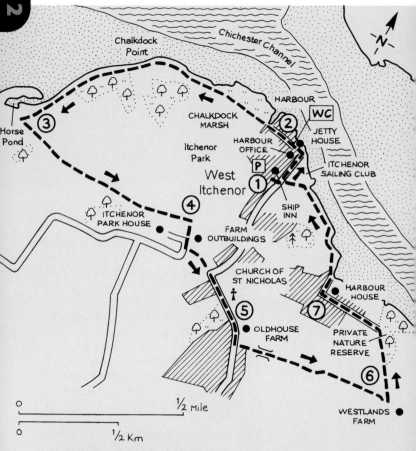

## Walk 12 Directions

① From the car park walk along to the road and bear left, heading towards the harbour front. Pass the **Ship Inn** and make your way down

to the water's edge. Look for the harbour office and the toilets and follow the footpath to the left of **Jetty House**.

② Cut between hedging and fencing to reach a boat yard and

then continue ahead on the clear country path. Keep left at the next junction and shortly the path breaks cover to run hard by the harbour and its expanses of mud flats. Cross **Chalkdock Marsh** and continue on the waterside path.

③ Keep going until you reach a footpath sign. Turn left here by a sturdy old oak tree and follow the path away from the harbour edge, keeping to the right-hand boundary of the field. Cross a stile to join a track on a bend and continue ahead, still maintaining the same direction. Pass **Itchenor Park House** on the right and approach some farm outbuildings.

④ Turn right by a brick and flint farm outbuilding and follow the path, soon merging with a concrete track. Walk ahead to the next junction and turn left by a white

gate, down to the road. Bear right here, pass the speed restriction sign and soon you reach the little **Church of St Nicholas**.

⑤ Follow the road along to **Oldhouse Farm** and then turn left at the footpath sign to cross a footbridge. Keep to the right of several barns and follow the path straight ahead across the field. Pass a line of trees and keep alongside a ditch on the right into the next field. The path follows the hedge line, making for the field corner. Ahead are the buildings of **Westlands Farm**.

⑥ Turn sharp left by the footpath sign and follow the path across the field. Skirt the woodland, part of a private nature reserve, and veer left at the entrance to **the Spinney**. Follow the residential drive to **Harbour House**.

⑦ Turn right just beyond it and follow the path along the edge of the harbour. Keep going along here until you reach **Itchenor Sailing Club**. Bear left and walk up the drive to the road. Opposite you should be the **Ship Inn**. Turn left to return to the car park.

# Beeding's Royal Escape Route

*Take a leisurely stroll through the peaceful Adur Valley to an historic bridge crossed by a fugitive king.*

| | |
|---|---|
| **•DISTANCE•** | 2¾ miles (4.4km) |
| **•MINIMUM TIME•** | 1hr 30min |
| **•ASCENT / GRADIENT•** | Negligible ▲▲▲ |
| **•LEVEL OF DIFFICULTY•** | 🚶 🚶 🚶 |
| **•PATHS•** | Riverside, field and village paths, some road, 10 stiles |
| **•LANDSCAPE•** | Adur Valley flood plain |
| **•SUGGESTED MAP•** | aqua3 OS Explorer 122 South Downs Way – Steyning to Newhaven |
| **•START / FINISH•** | Grid reference: TQ 185105 |
| **•DOG FRIENDLINESS•** | Take care on approach to Beeding Bridge and in Bramber |
| **•PARKING•** | Free car park at Bramber Castle |
| **•PUBLIC TOILETS•** | Bramber and Beeding |

## BACKGROUND TO THE WALK

Crossing Beeding Bridge, which is recorded in documents dating back to the reign of Henry III, it's worth stopping for a few moments to consider its importance as a river crossing. Not only does the bridge play a vital part in this walk, allowing you to cross the River Adur from one bank to the other, but 350 years ago, in October 1651, it enabled Charles II, defeated and on the run, to escape his enemies and eventually flee to France.

### Pursued by Parliament

His route through the Adur Valley was one step on a long and eventful journey that has became an integral part of British history. Following the Battle of Worcester, where his army was soundly beaten, the young Charles fled across England, hotly pursued by Parliamentary forces under the leadership of Oliver Cromwell. Though documented fact, it has all the hallmarks of a classic adventure story, a colourful, rip-roaring tale of intrigue and suspense.

First, he made his way north, intending to cross the River Severn into Wales where he could find a ship and sail to the continent. But the river was heavily guarded and Charles was forced to change his plans.

### Troopers on the Bridge

Instead he travelled south through the Cotswolds and the Mendips, eventually reaching Charmouth on the Dorset coast. Once again his plans to escape by boat fell through and, in a desperate attempt to avoid capture, he made his way along the South Coast to Shoreham near Brighton, where at last he found a ship which could take him to France. His journey through England lasted six weeks and during that crucial period he was loyally supported by his followers, many at great risk to their own lives.

The King's arrival in Bramber was one heart-stopping moment among many during his time on the run. As he and his escort came into the village from the west, they were horrified to find many troopers in the vicinity of the riverbank. Charles realised they had been posted here to guard Beeding Bridge, which was his only means of reaching Shoreham easily. Cautiously, he crossed the bridge and continued on his way undetected. Moments later, the Royal party looked round to see a group of cavalry hotly pursuing them across country. Charles feared the worst, but as they reached him, the soldiers suddenly overtook the King and rode off into the distance. Fortunately for Charles, they had been pursuing someone else on that occasion. After their narrow escape in the Adur valley, the group decided it was safer to split up and make their own way to the coast.

The accent is firmly on history on this very pleasant valley walk. Making for the Adur, the route follows the river to the bridge which Charles II crossed in the middle of the 17th century. The walk continues south by the river before crossing farmland back to Bamber.

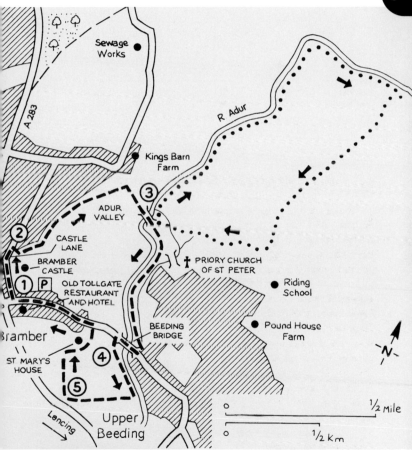

## Walk 13 **Directions**

① Follow the drive down to the roundabout. Turn right into **Castle Lane** and follow it through the woodland. On reaching the

junction with **Roman Road**, turn right to join a footpath.

② Head up through the trees, passing galvanised gates on the left and right. The rooftops of houses and bungalows peep into view

**Walk 13**

along here. Continue ahead at the next signpost and the **River Adur** can be glimpsed between the trees on the right. Pass a footpath on the left and make for a stile ahead. Follow the grassy path to the next stile and footpath sign. Cross over and turn right towards the footbridge spanning the **Adur**.

③ Cross the stile and bridge. Bear right, following the riverbank towards **Upper Beeding**. Branch off left to a footbridge and stile in order to visit the **Priory Church of St Peter**. Returning to the main walk, continue towards **Upper Beeding**. Cross a stile by a gate and continue to a kissing gate. Follow the path to the **Bridge Inn** at Beeding and cross the **Adur**.

④ Swing left and join the right-hand bank, heading downstream. Cross a stile and follow the riverside path. Continue to a right-hand stile and enter the field. Keep the hedge on the right and at the fence corner go straight on, out across the field.

⑤ As you approach the A283, turn right in front of the stile and head towards the trees, with the ruins of **Bramber Castle** peeping through.

> **WHAT TO LOOK FOR**
> Overlooking the Adur Valley and just off the walk is **Sele Priory**, which was established by William de Braose. Sele is simply another name for Beeding. The vicarage now occupies the site of the old priory, part of an ancient Benedictine foundation, and next to it is the Priory Church of St Peter.

Make for a stile and bear right. Follow the track as it bends left and crosses two stiles before joining a tarmac drive running through the trees to the road. Turn left, pass **St Mary's House** and walk along the **High Street**, passing the **Castle Inn Hotel**. On reaching the **Old Tollgate Restaurant** and hotel, cross the road and follow the steps up to the car park.

> **WHILE YOU'RE THERE**
> Before starting the walk, have a look at the ruins of **Bramber Castle** just a few paces from the car park. Now in the care of English Heritage and the National Trust, it was built just after the Norman Conquest to defend the exposed and vulnerable Sussex coast. The castle was held by the de Braose family until 1326 when it passed to Alice de Bohun and then to her eldest son. Later, during the Civil War, it was badly assaulted by the Roundheads. Nowadays, all that remains of it is the 70ft (21m) high gateway. At the centre of the site is evidence of a motte which might have borne a timber tower. Next to Bramber Castle is the **Parish Church of St Nicholas**, originally the castle chapel. Like the castle, this building also suffered in battle. Cromwell's men apparently used it as a gun emplacement, causing extensive damage to the nave and tower. Towards the end of the walk, you pass the entrance to **St Mary's House** in Bramber. This splendid medieval building is one of the village's proudest features and the best example of late 15th-century timber framing in Sussex. One of the highlights of a tour of the house is seeing the unique printed room, decorated for the visit of Queen Elizabeth I.

# The Snake River and the Seven Sisters

*Follow a breezy trail beside the Cuckmere River as it winds in erratic fashion towards the sea.*

| | |
|---|---|
| **·DISTANCE·** | 3 miles (4.8km) |
| **·MINIMUM TIME·** | 1hr 30min |
| **·ASCENT / GRADIENT·** | Negligible ▲▲▲ |
| **·LEVEL OF DIFFICULTY·** | 🚶🚶 🚶🚶 🚶🚶 |
| **·PATHS·** | Grassy trails and well-used paths. Mostly beside the Cuckmere or canalised branch of river |
| **·LANDSCAPE·** | Exposed and isolated valley and river mouth |
| **·SUGGESTED MAP·** | aqua3 OS Explorer 123 South Downs Way – Newhaven to Eastbourne |
| **·START / FINISH·** | Grid reference: TV 518995 |
| **·DOG FRIENDLINESS·** | Under close control within Seven Sisters Country Park. On lead during lambing season and near A259 |
| **·PARKING·** | Fee-paying car park at Seven Sisters Country Park |
| **·PUBLIC TOILETS·** | Opposite car park, by visitor centre |

## BACKGROUND TO THE WALK

One of the few remaining undeveloped river mouths in the south-east, is the gap or cove known as Cuckmere Haven. It is one of the south coast's best-known and most popular beauty spots and was regularly used by smugglers in the 18th century to bring ashore their cargoes of brandy and lace. The scene has changed very little in the intervening years with the eternal surge of waves breaking on the isolated shore.

The Cuckmere River joins the English Channel at this point but not before it makes a series of extraordinarily wide loops through lush water-meadows. It's hardly surprising that this characteristic has earned it the occasional epithet 'Snake River'. Winding ever closer to the sea, the Cuckmere emerges beside the famous white chalk cliffs known as the Seven Sisters. Extending east towards Birling Gap, there are, in fact, eight of these towering chalk faces, with the highest one, Haven Brow (253ft/77m), closest to the river mouth. On the other side of the estuary rise the cliffs of Seaford Head, a nature reserve run by the local authority.

### Seven Sisters Country Park

The focal point of the lower valley is the Seven Sisters Country Park, an amenity area of 692 acres (280ha) developed by East Sussex County Council. The site is a perfect location for a country park and has been imaginatively planned to blend with the coastal beauty of this fascinating area. There are artificial lakes and park trails, and an old Sussex barn near by has been converted to provide a visitor centre which includes many interesting exhibits and displays.

However, there is more to the park than these obvious attractions. Wildlife plays a key role within the park's boundaries, providing naturalists with many hours of pleasure and enjoyment. The flowers and insects found here are at their best in early to mid summer, while spring and autumn are a good time to bring your binoculars with you for a close-up view of migrant birds.

### A Haven for Birds

Early migrant wheatears are sometimes spotted in the vicinity of the river mouth from late February onwards and are followed later in the season by martins, swallows, whinchats and warblers. Keep a careful eye out for whitethroats, terns and waders too. The lakes and lagoons tend to attract waders such as curlews, sandpipers and little stints. Grey phalaropes have also been seen in the park, usually after severe autumn storms. These elusive birds spend most of their lives far out to sea, usually off South America or western Africa.

The walk explores this part of the Cuckmere Valley and begins by heading for the beach. As you make your way there, you might wonder why the river meanders the way it does. The meltwaters of the last Ice Age shaped this landscape and over the centuries rising sea levels and a freshwater peat swamp influenced the river's route to the Channel. Around the start of the 19th century, the sea rose to today's level and a new straight cut with raised banks, devised in 1846, shortened the Cuckmere's journey. This unnatural waterway controls the river and helps prevent flooding in the valley.

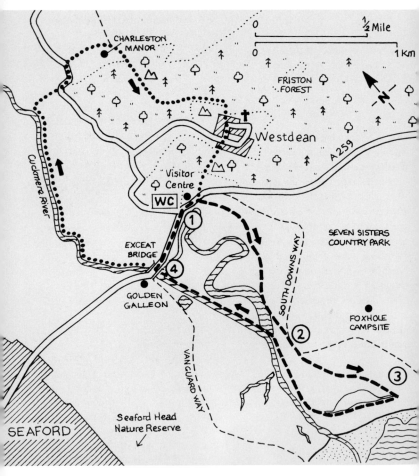

# Walk 14 **Directions**

① Make for the gate near the entrance to the **Seven Sisters Country Park** and follow the wide, grassy path towards the beach. The path gradually curves to the right, running alongside a concrete track. The **Cuckmere River** meanders beside you, heading for the open sea. Continue ahead between the track and the river and make for a **South Downs Way** sign.

> **WHERE TO EAT AND DRINK** ⓘ
> The **Golden Galleon** by Exceat Bridge is a popular 18th-century inn thought to have inspired Rudyard Kipling's poem *Song of the Smugglers*. The menu is traditional English, with various Italian, Oriental and Indian dishes. The ales are supplied by the pub's own micro-brewery. The visitor centre at the **Seven Sisters Country Park** has a restaurant and tea rooms and in summer there is often an ice cream van in the car park.

② Avoid the long distance trail as it runs in from the left, pass it and the **Foxhole campsite** and keep ahead, through the gate towards the beach. Veer left at the beach and **South Downs Way** sign. On reaching the next gate, don't go through it. Instead, keep right and follow the beach sign. Pass a couple of wartime pill boxes on the left, an evocative reminder of less peaceful times, and go through a gate. Join a stony path and walk ahead to the beach, with the white wall of the **Seven Sisters** rearing up beside you.

> **WHAT TO LOOK FOR** ⓘ
> Shingle plants thrive on the sheltered parts of beaches and a stroll at Cuckmere Haven reveals the yellow horned-poppy and the fleshy leaved sea kale. Sea beet, curled dock and scentless chamomile also grow here.

③ Turn right and cross the shore, approaching a **Cuckmere Haven Emergency Point** sign. Branch off to the right to join another track here. Follow this for about 50yds (46m) until you come to a junction and keep left, following the **Habitat Trail** and **Park Trail**. Keep beside the Cuckmere and the landscape here is characterised by a network of meandering channels and waterways, all feeding into the river. Pass a turning for **Foxhole campsite** and follow the footpath as it veers left, in line with the **Cuckmere**. Make for a kissing gate and continue on the straight path by the side of the river.

④ Keep ahead to the road at **Exceat Bridge** and on the left is the **Golden Galleon** pub. Turn right and follow the A259 to return to the car park at the country park.

> **WHILE YOU'RE THERE** ⓘ
> If you have the time, take a look at the **Seaford Head Nature Reserve**, which lies on the west side of Cuckmere Haven. This chalk headland, which rises 282 ft (85m) above the sea, is a popular local attraction and from here the coastal views are magnificent.

**Walk 15**

# How Rye Repelled the Enemy

*Wide skies, lonely seas and lagoons form the backdrop to this remote coastal walk, which is excellent for birdwatching.*

| | |
|---|---|
| •DISTANCE• | 4½ miles (7.2km) |
| •MINIMUM TIME• | 2hrs |
| •ASCENT / GRADIENT• | Negligible |
| •LEVEL OF DIFFICULTY• | |
| •PATHS• | Level paths and good, clear tracks, no stiles |
| •LANDSCAPE• | Mixture of shingle expanses and old gravel workings, now part of a local nature reserve |
| •SUGGESTED MAP• | aqua3 OS Explorer 125 Romney Marsh, Rye & Winchelsea |
| •START / FINISH• | Grid reference: TQ 942190 |
| •DOG FRIENDLINESS• | Dogs on leads within Rye Harbour Local Nature Reserve |
| •PARKING• | Spacious free car park at Rye Harbour |
| •PUBLIC TOILETS• | Rye Harbour |

## BACKGROUND TO THE WALK

Turn the clock back to the dark days of the World War II and you would find Rye Harbour a very different place. Blockhouses for machine guns littered the coast and barbed wire and landmines made it a 'no go' area. During the hours of darkness great searchlights swept across the night sky; they were particularly effective detecting the dreaded flying bombs. Go there now and you can still identify some of these crumbling relics of war. It's a fascinating exercise to rewrite the pages of history and imagine what might have happened if enemy forces had landed on this forgotten corner of England.

**Napoleonic Threat**

But this wasn't the first time the area had been under threat. During the Napoleonic Wars, 150 years earlier, Rye Harbour was considered an obvious target for invasion and attack when the Martello tower, seen by the car park at the start of the walk, became the first of 47 fortifications built in Sussex as a defence against the French. The tower would certainly have been a tough deterrent. The walls are nearly 12ft (4m) thick at the base and the middle floor would have been occupied by a garrison of one officer and 24 men.

Since then, the sea has built up over ½ mile (800m) of land in front of it, with violent storms dumping huge deposits of shingle on the shore every winter. Today, the little community of Rye Harbour is peaceful and yet, years after the shadows of war have passed over, it still conveys that same sense of bleak isolation. Though not as atmospheric as neighbouring, shingle-strewn Dungeness, it does feel isolated from the rest of the country.

Part of a designated Site of Special Scientific Interest (SSSI), Rye Harbour Local Nature Reserve lies at the mouth of the River Rother, which forms its eastern boundary. During its early stages, the walk follows the river and at first glance the shingle seems so bare and inhospitable that it is hard to imagine any plant could grow here. But in late May and June the beach is transformed by a colourful array of flowers. Delicate yellow horned poppies, sea kale, carpets of seaweed and countless other species of plants thrive in this habitat. Salt marsh, vegetation along the river's edge, pools and grazing marsh add to the variety and the old gravel pits now represent an important site for nesting terns, gulls, ducks and waders. Rye Harbour is best known for its bird life and very popular with ornithologists.

The walk follows the coast for some time, passing the Ternery Pool, originally two separate gravel workings dug by hand early in the 20th century. It continues along the coast before heading inland to some more flooded gravel pits. Here you might easily spot gulls, grebes, cormorants, swallows and reed warblers. Turtle doves are often seen in the fields and sometimes perch in pairs on the overhead wires.

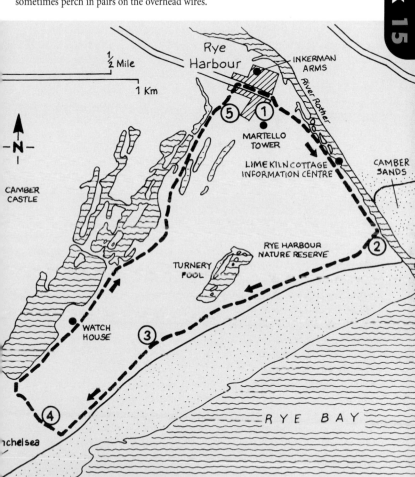

## Walk 15 Directions

① Keep the **Martello Tower** and the entrance to the holiday village on your right and enter **Rye Harbour Local Nature Reserve**. The **Rother** can be seen on the left, running parallel to the path. Head for **Lime Kiln Cottage** information centre and continue on the firm path, with the Rother still visible on the left. The sprawling expanse of **Camber Sands**, a popular holiday destination, nudges into view beyond the river mouth.

**Walk 15**

② Follow the path to the beach, then retrace your steps to the point where a permissive path runs off to the left, cutting between wildlife sanctuary areas where access is not allowed. Pass the entrance to the **Guy Crittall hide** on the right. From here there are superb views over **Turnery Pool**. In the distance, Rye's jumble of houses can be seen sprawling over the hill. Continue west on the clear path and gradually it edges nearer the shore.

---

**WHAT TO LOOK FOR** ⓘ

The **little tern** is one of Rye Harbour's summer visitors. Arriving in April, it stays until September when it departs for its wintering grounds on the African coast. Several eggs are laid in May on bare shingle or sand along the coast. The best colonies are found in protected areas controlled by wardens. Through their efforts, the populations of these terns have increased in recent years.

---

③ Ahead now is the outline of the old abandoned **lifeboat house** and, away to the right in the distance, the unmistakable profile of **Camber Castle**. Keep going on the clear path until you reach a waymarked footpath on the right, running towards a line of houses on the eastern edge of **Winchelsea**.

---

**WHERE TO EAT AND DRINK** ⓘ

The **Inkerman Arms** at Rye Harbour specialises in seafood and locally caught fresh fish. Food is available both at lunchtime and in the evening. Also in Rye Harbour, the **William the Conqueror** pub serves food and nearby **Bosun's Bite** café offers a range of sandwiches, baguettes and burgers.

---

④ Take this footpath and head inland, passing a small pond on the right. Glancing back, the old lifeboat house can be seen standing out starkly against the sky. Turn right at the next junction, pass the **Watch House** and continue on the track as it runs alongside several lakes. Pass to the left of some dilapidated farm outbuildings and keep going along the track. The lakes are still seen on the left-hand side, dotted with trees, and the silent, motionless figures of fishermen can often be seen along here. Begin the approach to **Rye Harbour** and on the left is the spire of the church.

⑤ On reaching the road in the centre of the village, turn left to visit the parish church before heading back along the main street. Pass the **Inkerman Arms** and return to the car park.

---

**WHILE YOU'RE THERE** ⓘ

Stop and look at the **old lifeboat station** beside the route of the walk. It's not been used since one stormy night in November 1928 when the 17-strong crew of the *Mary Stanford* were called to rescue a leaking steamer in the English Channel. The volunteers ran from their beds and dragged the lifeboat into the sea through gale force winds and huge waves. Soon afterwards, the coastguard heard the steamer was safe but with no ship-to-shore radio available he was unable to convey a message to the lifeboat crew. The next day, the *Mary Stanford* was seen floating upside down in the water. Not one volunteer survived the tragedy. Today the old building lies empty, abandoned and forlorn – in keeping with its surroundings. The churchyard at Rye Harbour has a memorial to the crew of the *Mary Stanford*.

Walk 16

# Butterflies Over Dover

*An exhilarating trail over Dover's famous white cliffs.*

| | |
|---|---|
| •DISTANCE• | 5½ miles (8.8km) |
| •MINIMUM TIME• | 2hrs 30min |
| •ASCENT / GRADIENT• | 131ft (40m) ▲▲▲ |
| •LEVEL OF DIFFICULTY• | 🚶🚶 🚶 |
| •PATHS• | Chalky cliff paths, some sections of road |
| •LANDSCAPE• | Grassy clifftops with extensive sea views |
| •SUGGESTED MAP• | aqua3 OS Explorer 138 Dover, Folkestone & Hythe |
| •START / FINISH• | Grid reference: TR 321412 |
| •DOG FRIENDLINESS• | Good, but best to start from clifftop car park with a dog |
| •PARKING• | Russell Street and St James Lane, also on cliffs by National Trust tea room |
| •PUBLIC TOILETS• | Dover and National Trust tea room |

## BACKGROUND TO THE WALK

Go on, admit it. As soon as you saw that this walk took you over those famous white cliffs you came over all Vera Lynn and hummed, 'There'll be bluebirds over the white cliffs of Dover,' to yourself. It's okay, practically everyone who walks here does the same at some point. Yet while this distinctive landmark is known all over the world and is seen as a symbol of England, few people realise that it is also an important wildlife habitat – so important that it supports species that are rarely found elsewhere in the country.

### The Chalk Downland

The cliffs, which are made of chalk, are topped with a thin, porous soil that has been grazed by animals for hundreds of years, creating what is known as chalk downland. Grazing stops coarse grasses and scrub invading the land and creates the ideal environment for hundreds of wild flowers to flourish. And while the early farmers didn't realise it, they were creating unique plant communities. While you're walking, keep your eyes peeled for plants like horseshoe vetch, early spider orchid and yellow rattle that gets its name from the seed pods that rattle in the wind. And with wild flowers, of course, come butterflies – particularly those wonderful blue ones that you so rarely see these days. Look out for the silvery chalkhill blue and the gorgeous sapphire Adonis blue. I even spotted a butterfly here in December. It wasn't close enough to identify, but it was a cheering sight nonetheless.

### Grazing Ponies

Other wild creatures of the cliffs include adders (you're unlikely to see one, they hide from people), slow worms (not a snake but a legless lizard), common lizards and birds such as fulmars, peregrine falcons and skylarks – no bluebirds though.

Unfortunately modern farming methods have led to a 98 per cent decline in chalk downland and with it, of course, a similar decline in the plants and animals it supports. In an attempt to halt this decline, the National Trust has introduced Exmoor ponies to the white cliffs. These hardy little ponies eat the coarse grasses that would otherwise invade the land, and so allow the wild flowers to grow.

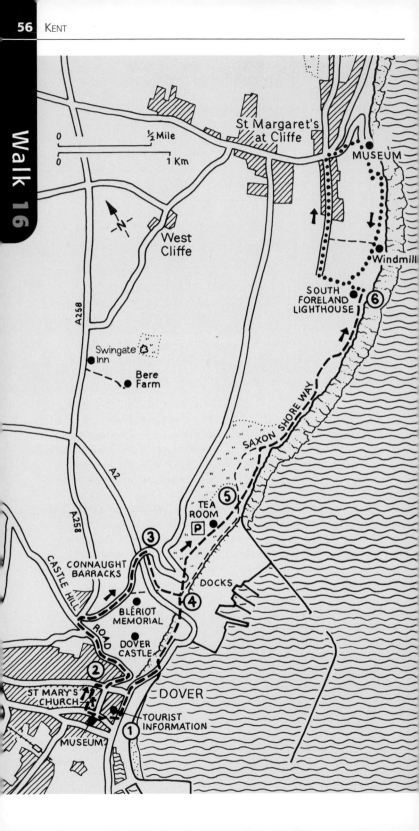

St Margaret's at Cliffe

MUSEUM

West Cliffe

Windmill

SOUTH FORELAND LIGHTHOUSE

⑥

A258

Swingate Inn

Bere Farm

SAXON SHORE WAY

A2

A258

⑤

TEA ROOM
P

③

CONNAUGHT BARRACKS

DOCKS

BLÉRIOT MEMORIAL

④

DOVER CASTLE

CASTLE HILL ROAD

②

ST MARY'S CHURCH

DOVER

MUSEUM

① TOURIST INFORMATION

0      ½ Mile

0      1 Km

N

# Walk 16 Directions

① From the **tourist information centre** on the front, walk to the right and at a roundabout go up **Bench Street**. At a crossing turn left into the market square. **Dover Museum** is just to the left. Turn up the road on the right. Keep going to **St Mary's Church** and then turn right along the path that runs beside the church. Keep ahead through the car park, cross some water and come out on to **Maison Dieu Road**.

### WHILE YOU'RE THERE
**Dover Castle** was built by the Normans after the Conquest in 1066 to control the native population. But the site, high above the sea, has an even more ancient history. There was an Iron-Age hill fort here and the Romans used the site to defend this part of their empire. Inside the castle you can see the remains of the Pharos, a beacon, which helped to guide the Roman fleet into the harbour.

② Turn right here, and then left, steeply, up **Castle Hill Road**. Eventually pass the entrance to **Dover Castle**. Further on, just past **Connaught Barracks**, turn right along Upper Road, signed 'Blériot Memorial'.

③ Cross the bridge over the main road and then take the footpath on the right. Go down some steps, fork left and, in a few paces, fork right.

Continue on this track and eventually emerge from the scrub to see the sea.

④ Turn left here, walk up some steps, with docks on your right. At a National Trust car park follow the **Saxon Shore Way** down to the right and over the cliffs. Continue past the coastguard station to a gate.

⑤ The path now continues along the cliffs and up to **South Foreland Lighthouse**. Some of the tracks branch off and lead very close to the cliffs – but there is a danger of cliff falls so keep to the main route. You may see some Exmoor ponies on this part of the walk. They've been introduced to the cliffs to graze the rare chalk downland and help preserve the habitat.

⑥ At **South Foreland Lighthouse** turn around and retrace your steps along the cliff – no hardship when you have these views. You can take the upper path here and walk past the **National Trust tea room** if you fancy stopping for tea. Otherwise continue down the steps and walk under the main road. Go along **Athol Terrace**, past the **First and Last** pub, and up on to the main road and back to the start point.

### WHERE TO EAT AND DRINK ⓘ
The **National Trust tea room** on the cliffs is the best place to stop. You can get tea, scones and cakes or something more substantial, like a hot sandwich.

### WHAT TO LOOK FOR ⓘ
Early on in this walk you'll pass a sign for the **Blériot Memorial** and, as it's only a short distance off the main route, it's worth a visit. The memorial commemorates the first successful flight across the English Channel. The *Daily Mail* set a challenge to early aviators offering £1,000 to the first person who could cross the Channel by plane. The prize was won by Frenchman Louis Blériot (1872–1936), who flew from France on 25 July 1909 in a single-engined plane and crash-landed not far from Dover Castle. The flight lasted 37 minutes.

# Three Mills and the Canals

*Discover the history of the East End waterways on this tow path walk.*

| | |
|---|---|
| **·DISTANCE·** | 4¼ miles (6.8km) |
| **·MINIMUM TIME·** | 2hrs 30min |
| **·ASCENT / GRADIENT·** | Negligible |
| **·LEVEL OF DIFFICULTY·** | |
| **·PATHS·** | Gravel, tarmac and tow paths |
| **·LANDSCAPE·** | Mainly canalside industry and housing |
| **·SUGGESTED MAP·** | aqua3 OS Explorers 162 Greenwich & Gravesend; 173 London North |
| **·START / FINISH·** | TQ 383828; near Bromley-by-Bow tube (on Explorer 173) |
| **·DOG FRIENDLINESS·** | No particular problems |
| **·PARKING·** | Tesco car park, Three Mill Lane; Bromley-by-Bow tube ¼ mile (400m) |
| **·PUBLIC TOILETS·** | At car park |

## BACKGROUND TO THE WALK

In the mid 19th century the banks of the River Lea were lined with flourishing industries. At that time, because it was deemed to be outside the City of London with its stringent pollution regulations, the water and surrounding air quality were dangerously poor. Since the demise of canal transport, this area, which is just a few steps away from hectic everyday life, has been transformed into a clean, peaceful haven for both walkers and wildlife.

### Life Along the Lea

In the 14th century Edward III instigated a policy to encourage commercial expansion, which led to the manufacture of gunpowder, paper, soap, flour and porcelain along the Lea. These were vibrant times, but it wasn't until the 1700s that work was carried out on the meandering river to construct straight channels and build locks so that freight could be transported more easily. Some parts of east London were more significant than others in the development of the chemical industry. West Ham, for example, was just outside the jurisdiction of the Metropolitan Buildings Act of 1844 that protected the City from anti-social trades such as oil-burning and varnish making. Industry developed in Bromley-by-Bow because there was lots of cheap land and no building restrictions.

### The Demise of the Waterways

As the Industrial Revolution progressed in the 19th century, the River Lea became an enormous health hazard. The factories along its banks produced a great deal of waste – the river was, in effect, used as a dumping ground for chemical and pharmaceutical waste. Looking at the scene before you today, it's not easy to picture a skyline of mass industrialism. Warehouses, cranes and gas works were here, against a backdrop of smoggy, smelly air. But, together with the noise of the powerful machinery, this would have been a way of life for many workers. For more than half of the 20th century barges still brought raw materials to the factories from London Docks, taking away the finished goods. Today, however, you're more likely to see a heron than a vessel on this stretch of the river.

Hackney Wick

Sta

STRATFORD

A 106

A 102 (M)

BOTTOM LOCK

③

VICTORIA PARK

MIDDLE LOCK

A 106

OLD FORD LOCK

A 115

A 11

WATTON HOUSE

A 1205

HERTFORD UNION CANAL

TOP LOCK

RIVER LEA

THREE MILLS GREEN

PUMPING STATION

④

B 119

BOW

FAT CAT CAFÉ

REGENTS CANAL

A 12

MATCH FACTORY (BRYANT & MAY)

②

MILL HOUSE

TESCO

THREE MILLS STUDIOS

A 11

MILE END LOCK

Mile End

Bromley

①

BOW LOCKS

JONSON LOCK

RAGGED SCHOOL MUSEUM

Devons Road Sta

⑥

-N-

A 11

B 140

B 140

LIMEHOUSE CUT

A 102

SALMON LOCK

A 1205

¼ Mile

LIBRARY

A 13

½ Km

A 13

Limehouse Station

⑤

A 13

# Walk 17 Directions

① From the Tesco supermarket car park in **Three Mills Lane** take the footpath to the left of an iron bridge marked 'Lee Navigation Tow Path' and 'Bow Flyover'. Continue walking ahead with the river to your right-hand side and you will shortly see the formidable volume of traffic coming into view, going across the Bow Flyover.

② Where the path ends walk up the ramp on your left, leading to the **A12**. Turn right, cross the **A11** ahead of you and turn right at the railings. Now walk down the slope and across a bridge to rejoin the tow path, with the river now to your left. Notice the brickwork of the old Bryant & May **match factory** ahead to your left. The path swings right, away from the traffic. Ignore the Greenway sign on the right and pass under two pipes that are part of the old Victorian sewer. Cross a bridge and continue along the **River Lea**, past the **Old Ford Lock**.

③ Just before the next bridge ahead, the **Hertford Union Canal** emerges and joins at a right angle on the left. Cross the bridge and turn left down a slope to join this canal along a gravel path. Pass **Bottom Lock**, **Middle Lock** and, further on, **Top Lock**. Once past the cottages of Top Lock, **Victoria Park** is visible on the right. Continue along this long, straight, paved path until you pass under **Three Colts Bridge**, a metal gate, two further bridges and another metal gate.

> **WHERE TO EAT AND DRINK** ⓘ
>
> At the footbridge joining the Regent's Canal is Bow Wharf where you'll find the **Fat Cat Café and Bar**. A converted builders' yard, it has outside, daytime seating and a wooden interior with Chesterfield sofas. A good selection of wines, and beers include IPA and Spitfire.

④ Cross a footbridge at this T-junction of the waterways to pick up the southern section of the **Regent's Canal**, which was opened in 1820 and used by horse-drawn barges to haul coal through London. Continue along the canal, towards the blinking light of Canary Wharf. Pass under a railway bridge, **Mile End Lock**, two more bridges and **Jonson Lock**. Pass a red brick chimney, which is a sewer

> **WHILE YOU'RE THERE** ⓘ
>
> The **Ragged School Museum** in Copperfield Road was one of 148 schools set up by Dr Barnardo to educate poor children in London. The museum highlights the history of the East End, with a Victorian schoolroom taster session for children.

ventilation shaft, and walk under a railway bridge. Continue past **Salmon Lock** and notice the viaduct ahead. After walking under **Commercial Road Bridge**, turn left and follow the steps to the road.

⑤ Turn right along **Commercial Road** and pass **Limehouse Library** and a small park on the right. Ignore the first gate on the right and instead pass over a bridge and take the steps on the right-hand side that lead down to the canal. Turn right and follow the tow path of the canal, the **Limehouse Cut**, with the water on your left. A few paces further on pass under the **A13**. Follow the tarmac path under three more bridges until it leads on to the **A102**. Walk along the pavement for 50yds (46m) and cross the road using the underpass ahead of you.

⑥ Turn right, walking with the flow of traffic, and take the first road on the left to pick up the canal path at **Bow Locks**. Walk over the concrete footbridge and under two bridges. Continue ahead towards the **Mill House**. Turn left over the bridge back to the start.

> **WHAT TO LOOK FOR** ⓘ
>
> A Swedish manufacturer of matchsticks sold the British patent to Mr Bryant and Mr May who, in 1855, leased the **factory**, Bryant & May. A medical condition called 'phossy jaw' was common among workers and was often fatal. The fumes from the yellow phosphorous in the head of the match caused the jawbone to rot away – the smell from the diseased bone was apparently horrendous. In 1911 a new factory was built on the site; the remains have been converted into luxury flats.

# Wanstead and its Royal Connections

*Through Wanstead Park, where Robert Dudley, the Earl of Leicester, entertained Elizabeth I.*

| | |
|---|---|
| •DISTANCE• | 4¾ miles (7.7km) |
| •MINIMUM TIME• | 2hrs 30min |
| •ASCENT / GRADIENT• | Negligible ▲▲▲ |
| •LEVEL OF DIFFICULTY• | 𝕏𝕏 𝕏𝕏 𝕏𝕏 |
| •PATHS• | Mainly lakeside tracks that can get muddy |
| •LANDSCAPE• | Ornamental lake and parkland |
| •SUGGESTED MAP• | aqua3 OS Explorer 174 Epping Forest & Lee Valley |
| •START / FINISH• | Grid reference TQ 406882; Wanstead tube |
| •DOG FRIENDLINESS• | Keep on lead on roads to park |
| •PUBLIC TOILETS• | By Temple |

## BACKGROUND TO THE WALK

The surprising thing about Wanstead Park in east London is that, despite its close proximity to the North Circular road, the distant hum of traffic is really only noticeable from the northern side of the park. This is a lovely walk, enchanting even, for it traces the outline of the ornamental waters and its Grotto and Temple as well as Florrie's Hill. No wonder Elizabeth I kept returning.

### An Estate Like No Other

Wanstead has been associated with royalty ever since 1553 when Queen Mary, a Catholic, broke her journey here from Norwich to meet her sister, Princess Elizabeth, a Protestant, who rode out to Wanstead accompanied by hundreds of knights on horseback. The estate had belonged to Sir Giles Heron but, because he would not denounce his Catholic beliefs, Henry VIII (the girls' father) took it from him. After Mary's death, Elizabeth became Queen – she was just 25 years old. The estate at Wanstead then belonged to Robert Dudley, the Earl of Leicester, who had enlarged and improved the mansion. The two became very close and Dudley held some extremely lavish parties for his royal guest. In 1578 Elizabeth stayed in Wanstead for five days and no doubt would have spent some time walking in the wonderful grounds.

### Highs and Lows

When Queen Elizabeth died, James I succeeded her. In 1607 he spent the autumn in Wanstead. The manor was later sold to Sir James Mildmay. Unfortunately, as Mildmay was one of the judges at the trial of Charles I, which led to Charles' execution, the manor was taken from the family after the restoration and handed to the Crown. In 1667 Sir Josiah Child (whose family were the first private bankers in England) bought the manor and made huge improvements. Later, his son, Sir Richard, replaced the manor house and landscaped the gardens. Constructed using Portland stone, the front of the new mansion had a portico of six Corinthian columns. The building was considered one of the finest in the country, even rivalling Blenheim Palace. The Grotto was erected and the ornamental waters and lakes were also designed at this time. But why, you might ask, is there no mansion today? The blame lies chiefly with Catherine Tilney-Long, who inherited the extremely valuable property in 1794. Despite no shortage of admiring males, she married a gambling man, who took just ten years to blow her entire fortune. To pay off her husband's debts Catherine auctioned the contents of the house and, because a buyer could not be found for the house itself, the magnificent property was pulled down and sold in separate lots. Fortunately for us, despite this sad tale of decline, the wonderful grounds can still be enjoyed.

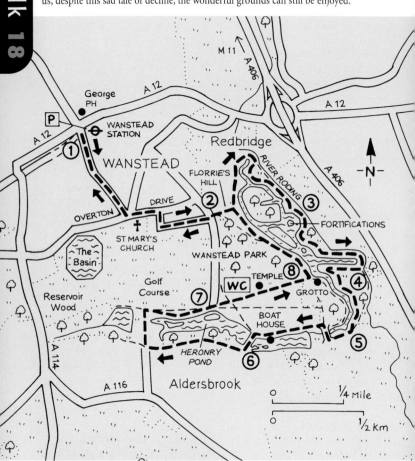

# Walk 18 **Directions**

① Turn left outside **Wanstead tube** into **The Green**, which becomes **St Mary's Avenue**. At the end cross the road into **Overton Drive**, which runs to the left of **St Mary's Church**. After the Bowls and Golf Club turn right, into **The Warren**

**Drive**. (The building on the right, before the road bends, was once the stable block and coach house to Wanstead House.)

② At the T-junction turn left and, almost immediately, enter **Wanstead Park** through the gate opposite. Continue ahead downhill (**Florrie's Hill**) to reach the

**Walk 18**

ornamental water. Follow the path to the left of the water and continue ahead as it runs to the right of the **River Roding**.

③ After another ¼ mile (400m) the path swings sharply to the left round an area known as the **Fortifications**, once a group of eight islands used for storing ammunition for duck-shooting and now a bird sanctuary. Soon after this the path traces the outline of a section of the water shaped like a finger. To your left are the steep banks of the **River Roding**.

④ At a meeting of paths turn right to continue alongside the water. When the path bends to the left, you will see the **Grotto** ahead.

⑤ At the T-junction turn right. At the end of the water turn right again, to cross a footbridge; then take the left-hand fork towards a field. At a crossing of paths keep ahead until you reach a boathouse. Turn left here and go out through the gate.

⑥ Immediately turn right to pick up a path leading to **Heronry Pond**, which narrows and passes over a mound. At a crossing of paths turn

right and keep ahead across the grass. At the next junction turn sharp right, towards the trees.

⑦ The path weaves around the pond to reach a metal gate. Go through this and take a left-hand fork to join a wide, grassy track lined with sweet chestnut trees. At the front of the Temple take the well-defined path on your right. A few paces further on turn left and continue on this path alongside the **Temple**. Keep ahead, ignoring the next path on the right.

⑧ When you reach the metal enclosure that surrounds the Grotto turn sharp left, as if you are going back on yourself, but, a few paces further on, take a footpath that veers right and hugs the water's edge before joining another, wider path. Turn next left up **Florrie's Hill** to retrace your steps back to **Wanstead tube**.

**Walk 19**

# Along the Thames to the Gardens at Kew

*View the famous Royal Botanic Gardens at Kew from a surprisingly peaceful stretch of the Thames Path.*

| | |
|---|---|
| •DISTANCE• | 7½ miles (12.1km) |
| •MINIMUM TIME• | 3hrs |
| •ASCENT / GRADIENT• | Negligible ▲▲ ▲ |
| •LEVEL OF DIFFICULTY• | 🚶 🚶 🚶 |
| •PATHS• | Mainly tow paths and tarmac |
| •LANDSCAPE• | Riverside gardens and pubs |
| •SUGGESTED MAP• | aqua3 OS Explorer 161 London South |
| •START / FINISH• | Grid reference: TQ 192767; Kew Gardens tube |
| •DOG FRIENDLINESS• | No problems (guide dogs only inside Kew Gardens) |
| •PUBLIC TOILETS• | Syon House |

## BACKGROUND TO THE WALK

Kew Gardens began life as a royal front lawn for Kew Palace, where George III lived during his years of mental illness. The collection of exotic plants here was started in the 1740s. Nearly a century later, in 1841, Queen Victoria handed the 300 acre (122ha) site to the nation as a public research institute. Since then it has grown from strength to strength, and is now the world's leading botanical research centre. Although this walk allows a glimpse along its boundaries, a visit inside is highly recommended, for which you should allow a few extra hours.

### Green Fingers

With the largest, living plant collection in the world, you'd expect there to be a lot of green fingers at Kew Gardens and there are. In fact 200 horticultural staff are responsible for mowing the lawns, looking after the tropical plants in the glasshouses and the Herbarium, where more than 6 million specimens of dried plants and fungi are stored. There are a further 100 scientists studying the medicinal importance of plants and many others based at one of the most visited parts of Kew, the Palm House.

### From the Outside Looking In

Depending on the time of the year, you may be able to see part of the Rhododendron Dell from the Thames Path. The river provides these spectacular shrubs with the humidity they love and although the soil is not naturally favourable, it has been treated with high-acidity mulch and sulphur to reduce the pH level. Rhododendrons are native to the Himalayas and were introduced to this country by the intrepid Victorians in the 1850s. There are now over 700 specimens of hardy species and hybrids in this Dell, some of which are unique to Kew Gardens. Flowering can extend from November to August but the best time to see the vivid array is late May.

Further along the Thames Path is the Syon Vista, an opening that affords views of the long, straight avenue leading to the Palm House. In keeping with the Victorian love of all things iron, the entire structure was built of iron and filled in with curved glass. However, in the mid 1980s it was deemed necessary to conduct some major restoration work and all the plants were removed and taken to a temporary home. It was not an easy task and the oldest pot plant in the world, the *Encephalartos altensteinii*, was enclosed in a special scaffold to avoid damage.

The Palm House contains a tropical rainforest where plants are divided into three sections: African, American, and Asia and the Pacific. A central area displays the tallest palm trees. If you decide to visit, you'll see not only some rare tropical plants but also ones that are now actually extinct elsewhere.

**Walk 19**

# Walk 19 Directions

① From the tube, follow the road ahead past the row of shops and turn right along **Sandycombe Road**, which becomes **Kew Gardens Road** as it bends to the left. At the main road opposite the **Royal Botanic**

**Gardens**, turn right and continue ahead to the traffic lights. Cross **Kew Green** and head towards the church on the green.

② Take the path to the left of **St Anne's Church**, which was built for Queen Anne in 1714, and with your back to the church columns follow the main path to the right. Once across the green, continue along **Ferry Lane** which leads to the **Thames Path**.

③ Turn left here following the river along an attractive stretch of the path that borders **Kew Gardens** and offers the outsider a tempting view of the famous botanic gardens from the other side of a formidable ivy-clad walled ditch.

④ Just after a field, cross a ditch with metal gates to the left, signifying that this is the boundary of the **Old Deer Park**, which is now the home of the Royal Mid-Surrey Golf Course. Continue walking ahead for a further mile (1.6km) on the obvious track and cross **Richmond Lock** to reach the other side of the Thames.

⑤ Follow the riverside path past a boatyard where the **Capital Ring path** veers away from the river to run by the **Twickenham Campus** of Brunel University. When you reach the road turn right and just past the convent, **Nazareth House**, turn right at a mini-roundabout, signposted 'Thames Path'.

⑥ Turn left alongside the river towards the popular chalet-style **Town Wharf** pub and here, bear left and turn first right into

**Church Street**. Go over a bridge, past the riverside **London Apprentice** pub. After a church the road swings to the left along **Park Road**. Enter **Syon Park** and follow the wide, tarmac road.

⑦ Exit the park via a walled path and turn right at the road. Cross a bridge and, if this path isn't flooded, turn right for a detour along the **Grand Union Canal**. Otherwise continue along the road ahead bearing right to go through **Watermans Park** and then rejoining the **Thames Path**.

⑧ Past an ever-present row of houseboats, turn right to cross **Kew Bridge**. Cross the road at a pedestrian crossing, continue ahead and bear left into **Mortlake Road**. Turn right into **Cumberland Road** and left at the end to retrace your steps along **Kew Gardens Road** back to the tube station at the start of the walk.

# Dorney Court and England's First Pineapple

*Visit one of Buckinghamshire's oldest houses and take a stroll by the Thames.*

| | |
|---|---|
| **•DISTANCE•** | 5 miles (8km) |
| **•MINIMUM TIME•** | 1hrs 45min |
| **•ASCENT / GRADIENT•** | Negligible |
| **•LEVEL OF DIFFICULTY•** | |
| **•PATHS•** | Roads, firm paths and Thames tow path |
| **•LANDSCAPE•** | Lowland Thames valley |
| **•SUGGESTED MAP•** | aqua3 OS Explorer 160 Windsor, Weybridge & Bracknell |
| **•START / FINISH•** | Grid reference: SU 938776 |
| **•DOG FRIENDLINESS•** | On lead in Dorney and under control by Thames |
| **•PARKING•** | Large car park at Dorney Common |
| **•PUBLIC TOILETS•** | None on route |

## BACKGROUND TO THE WALK

Located in Buckinghamshire's most southerly village, close to the Thames, Dorney Court prides itself on being a genuine medieval village manor house. Motorways and modern housing estates grow ever closer, but the Grade I listed house with its jumble of timber-framed gables has survived intact and unchanged for almost 600 years, looking much the same today as when it was first built.

### Fruit and Honey

The village of Dorney stands on a gentle rise in the Thames flood plain and is cut off from the river by spacious meadows where evidence of prehistoric life can be found in the damp peaty soil. The name Dorney means 'island of bumblebees' and the locally produced Dorney Court honey is renowned for its delicate, light flavours.

But it is not just honey for which the house is justly famous. The large carved stone pineapple standing in the corner of the Great Hall commemorates the first pineapple to be grown in England. The story suggests that the top of a pineapple, imported from Barbados, was sliced off at a dinner in the City of London and given to the Earl of Castlemaine's gardener to plant at Dorney Court. The pineapple thrived and was subsequently presented to Charles II in 1661. Nobody can be sure if it really happened but it makes a good story.

### Medieval Manor House

Back in the mid-1920s, *Country Life* described Dorney Court as 'one of the finest Tudor manor houses in England'. Few would dispute that label and what endears the house to so many people is its long tradition of continuous family occupation. In fact, Dorney Court has remained in the same family for over 450 years.

The first owner was recorded after the Norman Conquest and after changing hands several times in the 15th century, the house was sold in 1504 for the princely sum of 500 marks. By the middle of the 16th century the manor, together with 600 acres (243ha), was owned by Sir William Garrard, Lord Mayor of London. The Garrards were prosperous grocers, owning land in the Chalfonts area. It is through this family that the town of Gerrards Cross got its name. Sir William Garrard's daughter Martha married Sir James Palmer of Kent and Dorney Court has remained in the Palmer family to this day. One family portraits depicts Jane Palmer, who was born in 1564 and was a forebear of Diana, Princess of Wales. The layout of the house has changed little over the years, though since opening to the public in 1981 work has been undertaken to restore furniture and paintings.

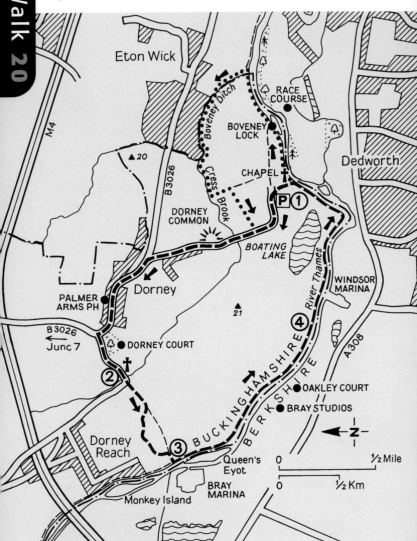

## Walk 20 **Directions**

① From the car park follow the road across **Dorney Common**, towards **Dorney** village. Pass

**Wakehams**, a timber-framed house with a well situated at the front, and away to the right is a fine view of Windsor Castle and its famous Round Tower. Keep left at the T-junction, cross a cattle grid and

Walk 20

join the pavement. Walk through Dorney, keeping the **Palmer Arms** on your right. Bear left into **Court Lane** and pass the entrance to **Dorney Court**. Follow the path parallel to the road and soon reach the **Church of St James the Less**.

② Continue on the path and when the road bends right, go straight ahead at the sign for **Dorney Lake, Park and Nature Reserve**. Keep to the right-hand side of the drive and follow the parallel path as it sweeps away to the right by a plaque and a grove of trees. Further on the path passes over a conveyor belt carrying sand and gravel from the nearby quarry works. Make for some trees and reach the **Thames Path** by a Sustrans waymark.

③ Turn left here and follow the national trail, keeping **Bray Marina** on the opposite bank. Further downstream the imposing cream

façade of **Bray film studios** edges into view, its sweeping riverside lawns and weeping willows enhancing the elegant scene. Continue on the leafy **Thames Path** and soon catch sight of **Oakley Court** across the water on the Berkshire bank.

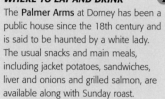

**WHERE TO EAT AND DRINK**
The **Palmer Arms** at Dorney has been a public house since the 18th century and is said to be haunted by a white lady. The usual snacks and main meals, including jacket potatoes, sandwiches, liver and onions and grilled salmon, are available along with Sunday roast.

④ Beyond the hotel can be seen the cabin cruisers and gin palaces of **Windsor Marina** and next to it lines of caravans and mobile homes overlooking the river. Through the trees on the Buckinghamshire bank is the outline of Eton College's new boathouse and its superb rowing lake. To gain a closer view, briefly follow a path beside the river boathouse and slipway, walk towards the lake and then retrace your steps to the **Thames Path**. On the opposite bank of the river is **Windsor Race Course Yacht Basin** and ahead now is the **Chapel of St Mary Magdalen**. Follow the path alongside the chapel to a kissing gate and about 50yds (46m) beyond it reach a lane. With the **Old Place** opposite and an avenue of chestnut trees on the right, turn left and return to the car park.

**WHILE YOU'RE THERE**
**Dorney Common**, still owned by the Lord of the Manor of nearby Dorney Court, has been managed in the same way since medieval times and some local residents are permitted to graze their animals here. After visiting Dorney Court, take time to look at the **Church of St James the Less** at Dorney, which dates from the 13th century. Note the Norman font, the 17th-century gallery, the Garrard tomb and the porch that was built in 1661 to celebrate the birth of Lady Anne Palmer.

**WHAT TO LOOK FOR**
With its Victorian Gothic façade, **Oakley Court** is an obvious choice for Hammer horror film producers – especially as it lies next door to Bray studios, home of Hammer. The house, now a hotel, has been used in various movie productions, including *The Curse of Frankenstein* (1957) and *The Rocky Horror Picture Show* (1975). The **Chapel of St Mary Magdalen** has been a place of worship since before the Norman Conquest. Parts of it date back to the 12th and 13th centuries and it may well have been used by boatmen when Boveney Lock was a bustling wharf transporting timber from Windsor Forest.

# A World of Water and Wildlife at Dinton Pastures

*This fascinating walk mostly stays within the boundaries of a popular country park, visiting six different lakes along the way.*

| | |
|---|---|
| •DISTANCE• | 3 miles (4.8km) |
| •MINIMUM TIME• | 1hr 30min |
| •ASCENT / GRADIENT• | Negligible |
| •LEVEL OF DIFFICULTY• | |
| •PATHS• | Lakeside and riverside paths, some road walking, no stiles |
| •LANDSCAPE• | Extensive lakeland |
| •SUGGESTED MAP• | aqua3 OS Explorer 159 Reading, Wokingham & Pangbourne |
| •START / FINISH• | Grid reference: SU 784718 |
| •DOG FRIENDLINESS• | Dogs under control and on lead where requested |
| •PARKING• | Large car park at Dinton Pastures |
| •PUBLIC TOILETS• | Dinton Pastures |

## BACKGROUND TO THE WALK

Dinton Pastures Country Park describes itself as a mosaic of rivers, meadows, lakes and woodland. The lakes were once gravel workings that were flooded to form the focal point of this attractive recreational area. Paths and self-guided trails enable visitors to explore this tranquil world of water and wildlife at will and, as you explore the park on foot, spare a thought to work out how it all began.

### The Early Days

The park's river meadows were once farmed by Anglo Saxons who called the area Whistley – 'wisc' meaning marshy meadow and 'lei', a wooded glade or clearing. The River Loddon was also used as part of the same process, farmed for its rich supply of eels, caught in willow traps for the monks of Abingdon Abbey. Traps were still in regular use as late as the 1930s.

By the beginning of the 17th century, much of the area formed part of Windsor Forest, where the Monarch and his courtiers indulged in hunting for pleasure. It was the courtiers who built some of the region's grandest houses, including High Chimneys, which was handy for Windsor Castle, the royal powerhouse. High Chimneys' farmhouse, which later became the Tea Cosy café, dates back to 1904. During the mid-1920s it was occupied by a farmer who named the farm after his home village of Dinton, near Aylesbury.

Dinton Pastures forms part of the Loddon's flood plain and is a rich source of gravel, which has been extracted here for more than 100 years. There was an extensive extraction programme here during the late 1960s and right through the 1970s. Much of the material was used to construct the M4 and the A329(M), connecting Reading and Wokingham.

### Recreational Area

Comprising about 230 acres (93ha) and officially opened to the public in 1979, Dinton Pastures attracts many visitors who come here to walk, fish, picnic and indulge in birdwatching – a welcome green space on Reading's doorstep. The largest of the lakes at

Dinton Pastures is Black Swan. The Emm Brook once flowed where the lake is now situated. It was later diverted and the oaks which you can see on the island in the lake were once on the banks of the old stream.

All the lakes draw a variety of wetland birds such as swans, geese, coots and moorhens. The park's rarest birds are bitterns – less than 20 pairs breed in Britain annually. Several fly here in winter and in spring migrants such as nightingales also make the journey from Africa to nest at Dinton Pastures. The park offers all sorts of surprises – you may spot a weasel or a stoat, catch sight of a mink in the Loddon, or identify one of 18 species of dragonfly in the lakes and rivers.

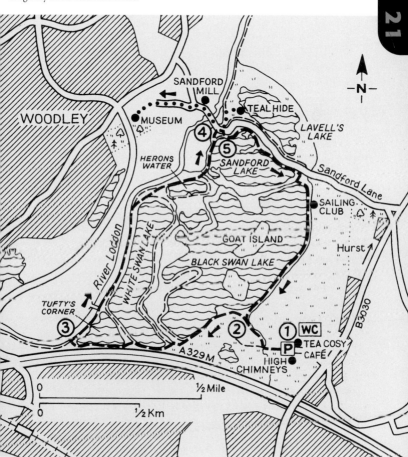

## Walk 21 **Directions**

① With the **Tea Cosy** café and Countryside Service office on the right and **High Chimneys** behind you, cross the car park to the large map of the site. Follow the wide path and keep right at the fork by the 'wildlife trails' sign. Pass an enclosed play area on the left, keep the **Emm Brook** on the right and enjoy the tantalizing glimpses of **Black Swan Lake** up ahead.

② Swing left on reaching the water and follow the path alongside the lake. When it veers right, turn left

Walk 21

across a bridge to a sign for Tufty's Corner. Bear right here and keep left at the fork after a few paces. Follow the path beside **White Swan Lake** to a waymark post by a patch of grass and a flight of steps. Avoid the steps but take the left-hand path and follow it to the lake known as **Tufty's Corner**. On reaching a junction by a bridge, turn right and keep the **River Loddon** on your left.

③ Walk along to the next bridge. Don't cross it; instead continue on the riverside path. White Swan Lake lies over to the right, glimpsed at intervals between the trees. Further on, the path curves to the right, in line with the river, before reaching a sign 'private fishing – members only'. Join a track on the right here and bear left. Pass alongside **Herons Water** to a sign 'Sandford Lake, Black Swan Lake and Lavell's Lake – Conservation Area'. Turn left and keep **Sandford Lake** on the right. When the path curves right, go out to the road.

④ To visit the **Berkshire Museum of Aviation**, bear left and pass **Sandford Mill**. Take the road signposted 'No Through Road' on the left, pass several cottages and continue ahead when the road dwindles to a path. The museum is on the left. Retrace your steps to Sandford Mill and keep walking ahead to a footpath and kissing gate on the left. Keep left at the first fork, then right at the second and head for the **Teal hide**. Return to the road, cross over and return to the lakeside path.

***WHAT TO LOOK FOR*** ⓘ
**Sandford Mill**, built in 1772, was in use until the mid-1950s and in 1994 it was converted into a private property. A mill was originally recorded on this site in the Domesday Book. With the trees surrounding it and its picturesque white weatherboarded façade, it creates a pretty picture in this corner of the park.

⑤ Continue with **Sandford Lake** on your right. On reaching a sign 'Sandford Lake – wildlife area – dogs under control' veer left over a bridge and turn left. **Black Swan Sailing Club** can be seen on the left. Continue on the broad path and look out across the lake to **Goat Island**, noted for its population of goats. On reaching the picnic area overlooking **Black Swan Lake**, turn left and retrace your steps back to the main car park.

***WHILE YOU'RE THERE*** ⓘ
Visit the **Teal Hide** at Lavell's Lake, overlooking the wader scrapes. See if you can spot wading birds from here – look out for the green sandpiper and redshank, ducks, swans, kingfishers and the occasional bittern. This site is for serious ornithologists. Not long ago this corner of the park was a meadow grazed by cattle or cut for hay, though the landscape changed dramatically at the time of gravel extraction. Take time to visit the **Berkshire Museum of Aviation**, just off the main route of the walk. The museum is dedicated to the contribution the county has made to flying. A Second World War hangar has been moved here from Woodley and there are various aircraft representing Berkshire's aviation history from the last 60 years or so.

# Secrets of Bletchley Park

*Puzzle over the enigma of Station X on this urban walk around Bletchley.*

| | |
|---|---|
| **·DISTANCE·** | 5 miles (8km) |
| **·MINIMUM TIME·** | 1hr 45min |
| **·ASCENT / GRADIENT·** | Negligble ▲▲▲ |
| **·LEVEL OF DIFFICULTY·** | 🏃🏃 🏃🏃 🏃🏃 |
| **·PATHS·** | Roads, park and field paths, canal tow path and riverside walk, 2 stiles |
| **·LANDSCAPE·** | Mixture of suburban streets and farmland |
| **·SUGGESTED MAP·** | aqua3 OS Explorer 192 Buckingham & Milton Keynes |
| **·START / FINISH·** | Grid reference: SP 868337 |
| **·DOG FRIENDLINESS·** | Under control in Blue Lagoon Park, along Broad Walk and by canal. Dogs are permitted in grounds of Bletchley Park |
| **·PARKING·** | Bletchley Station and approach road |
| **·PUBLIC TOILETS·** | Bletchley Station and Bletchley Park |

## BACKGROUND TO THE WALK

Bletchley Park. The name may sound ordinary enough but what took place here during the dark days of the Second World War is quite remarkable. This was the home of Station X – where more than 10,000 people worked in total secrecy in a small, nondescript town at the heart of the English shires.

### Brain Teasers

It was here that mathematicians, linguists, crossword enthusiasts and Oxbridge scholars battled for hours on end, in wooden huts and brick-built blocks, to break the seemingly unbreakable. Their role was to study the German military cipher machine, 'Enigma', and devise a programme to enable the Allies to decode the Nazis' secret radio messages, which often provided clues as to the enemy's next course of action. At times the code-breakers' task seemed impossible – after all, the odds against success were phenomenal. But they did succeed, shortening the war against Germany by as much as two years.

One of the key figures in the story of Bletchley Park was Alan Turing, a mathematical genius considered to be one of the pioneering fathers of the modern computer. It was he who invented the 'Bombe', an electro-mechanical machine of clattering code wheels intended to significantly reduce the time needed to break the daily-changing Enigma keys.

But why Bletchley Park? What was it about this Victorian mansion, built by a city financier, that made the men from British Intelligence choose it as their top secret Station X? Midway between the universities of Oxford and Cambridge and just a few minutes' walk from a mainline railway station with regular services to London and many other parts of the country, it seemed a perfect venue for the Government Code and Cypher School, which until then had been based at the Foreign Office. As the threat of war loomed, Bletchley Park was poised to become the key communications centre in the history of modern warfare.

In August 1939, code breakers arrived at Bletchley Park in large numbers. Their work had begun. They posed as members of 'Captain Ridley's shooting party' so as not to arouse suspicion in the area. Ridley was the man in charge of the school's move to Bletchley. For the next 40 years, no one outside Bletchley Park knew exactly what went on here, and so impeccable was the code breakers' professionalism that the Germans never even realised Enigma had been broken. Churchill called the staff at Bletchley Park his 'geese that laid the golden eggs but never cackled'.

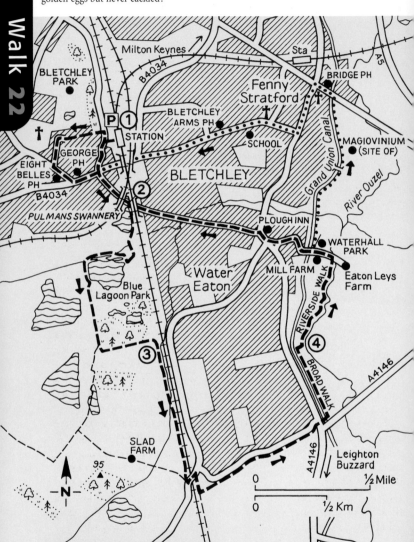

## Walk 22 Directions

① From the station car park cross the road and take the path to **Bletchley Park**. On leaving the former Station X walk along **Wilton Avenue** and left into **Church Green**

**Road**. Bear left at the junction with **Buckingham Road** and make your way towards Central Bletchley. Turn right into **Water Eaton Road**, pass beneath the Bletchley-to-Oxford railway line, and bear right at the footpath sign, just before the next railway bridge.

Walk 22

② Pass a pond, **Pulmans Swannery**, on the right and follow the fenced path to a stile. Continue to a fork, keep right and follow a track in an anti-clockwise direction round the edge of the lake. Avoid a ford and a footbridge and continue on the lakeside path. At the south west corner of the lake, look for some steps and a footbridge on the right. Turn left immediately beyond them and follow a path parallel to power lines. Bear left at a grassy track and follow it towards the railway line. Turn right immediately before a stile and keep to the right of a house. Swing left at a fence to reach a stile, and then walk ahead with the railway line on your left.

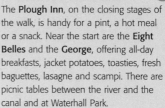

**WHERE TO EAT AND DRINK**
The **Plough Inn**, on the closing stages of the walk, is handy for a pint, a hot meal or a snack. Near the start are the **Eight Belles** and the **George**, offering all-day breakfasts, jacket potatoes, toasties, fresh baguettes, lasagne and scampi. There are picnic tables between the river and the canal and at Waterhall Park.

**WHAT TO LOOK FOR**
The **Grand Union Canal** is perfect for exploring on foot. The tow path provides excellent views of this historic waterway, originally known as the Grand Junction Canal. Its construction took place between 1793 and 1800, resulting in many changes to the landscape, but, more importantly, it provided work and business opportunities for local people.

③ Pass through a tunnel of trees and alongside farmland and, when you reach the drive to **Slad Farm**, exit to the road. Bear left, cross the railway bridge and turn immediately right at a gate. Follow the path for a short distance to a field corner and swing left to join a bridleway. Keep the houses of

Bletchley on your left, beyond the trees and hedgerow. On reaching the road, between two roundabouts, cross over to the canal bridge and swing left to follow the **Broad Walk**. At a sign for the **Riverside Walk**, turn right and then swing left after about 75yds (69m).

④ Keep the river a short distance away to the right. Draw level with a farm over to the right, cross a footbridge over a pond and turn left. Head for **The Watermill** and **Mill Farm**, avoiding the car park for **Waterhall Park**. Cross the bridge over the **Grand Union Canal** and keep right. Ahead now are several thatched and timber-framed cottages. Turn left in front of them and keep right at the main road junction, heading towards the **Plough** inn. Cross the road at the roundabout, following the sign for the station. Continue ahead through a residential area, pass beneath the two railway bridges seen near the start of the walk, go straight over at the junction and back to the station car park.

**WHILE YOU'RE THERE**
After the war the intelligence services continued to use part of the park as a training centre and the site was also used as a training college for teachers, post office workers and air traffic controllers. It was decommissioned in 1987 and in 1992 the **Bletchley Park Trust** was born to preserve the historic site. There's lots to see here so allow plenty of time for your visit. Props from the film *Enigma* (2001) are on display, the museum illustrates many Second World War activities and you can follow the Cryptology Trail, learning how messages were intercepted and delivered to Bletchley Park. Also on display is a replica of Colossus, the world's first programmable electronic computer.

# Abingdon's Architecture

*Explore a former county town and then view it from a classic riverside path.*

| | |
|---|---|
| •DISTANCE• | 7 miles (11.3km) |
| •MINIMUM TIME• | 2hrs 45min |
| •ASCENT / GRADIENT• | Negligible ▲▲▲ |
| •LEVEL OF DIFFICULTY• | 🚶 🚶 🚶 |
| •PATHS• | Field paths and tracks, stretches of road and Thames Path. Town and village streets (roads can be busy), 4 stiles |
| •LANDSCAPE• | Flat farmland and meadows south of Abingdon |
| •SUGGESTED MAP• | aqua3 OS Explorer 170 Abingdon, Wantage |
| •START / FINISH• | Grid reference: SU 503941 |
| •DOG FRIENDLINESS• | On lead in Sutton Courtenay; not ideal in Abingdon |
| •PARKING• | Small car park south of the church at Sutton Courtenay |
| •PUBLIC TOILETS• | Various, including Old Gaol Leisure Centre and Abbey Meadow Park |

## BACKGROUND TO THE WALK

From a distance, driving along the nearby A34, Abingdon doesn't look much. It's all business parks and out-of-town shopping centres. But leave the car behind, stroll its ancient streets and you'll be pleasantly surprised at what you find. Until 1867 Abingdon was the county town of Berkshire, later it was swallowed up when Oxfordshire greedily expanded her borders as part of the controversial county boundary changes of 1974.

The town was originally developed around its famous abbey, founded in AD 700 and dissolved in the reign of Henry VIII. The abbey was destroyed by the Danes in the 10th century, though work began to rebuild it and William the Conqueror spent Easter here in 1084. His son Henry I appointed the Italian Abbot Foritius in 1100 and the abbey was soon acknowledged as a symbol of power and prosperity. Some of the Abbey's outbuildings still remain today, including the Gateway, over which there was a room used as a prison until the 19th century.

Often compared to Oxford's magnificent Sheldonian Theatre, the splendid Old County Hall in the Market Place was completed in 1682 by Christopher Kempster of Burford, one of Wren's master masons during the building of St Paul's Cathedral. The Old County Hall is a perfect example of English Renaissance architecture – imposing and grand for such a small town. South of the Market Place is the Old Gaol built by Napoleonic prisoners of war between 1805 and 1811.

### A Soaring Landmark

The spire of the 15th-century St Helen's Church soars above the town and can be seen for miles around. The church, which is partly 13th-century, is 108ft (33m) wide and yet only 97ft (30m) long. Inside there are five aisles, a 200-year-old candelabra and a splendid medieval painted ceiling in the Lady Chapel, representing the Tree of Jesse.

Next door to the church are the Long Alley Almshouses. These comprise Long Alley, Brick Alley and Twitty's. The oldest, Long Alley, dates from the mid-15th century. The diarist Samuel Pepys came here in 1668 and put a donation in the almsbox.

Abingdon is very much a river town, with its buildings laid out along one bank of the Thames. From the meadows on the opposite bank it is reminiscent of a seaport, with all manner of sailing craft adding a dash of colour during the summer months.

Much of Abingdon's prosperity came from cloth manufacture and the historian John Leland noted in 1549 that the town 'standeth by clothing'. In more recent years the MG car plant provided Abingdon with regular employment until its eventual closure in the 1970s.

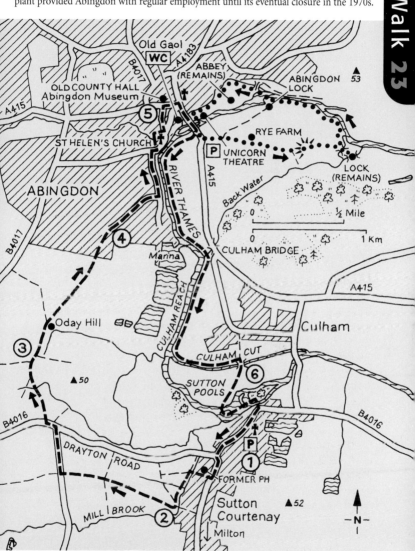

## Walk 23 **Directions**

① From the car park, turn left to the road, joining the adjacent tree-lined path. Take the turning for

Milton and follow the road to a former pub. Turn immediately right to join a footpath. Cross a footbridge to some cottages and swing left to a kissing gate. Keep left at the immediate fork and follow the path alongside the **Mill Brook**. Cross a double stile and a footbridge and continue to the next stile and footbridge.

② Turn right to join a track, following it between fields. Further on it narrows to a muddy path running between hedges. Make for the road, turn right, then bear left at the next junction, following **Drayton Road**. Take the second signposted right of way on the right.

**WHILE YOU'RE THERE**
Visit **Abingdon Museum**, which occupies the Old County Hall. As well as local archaeology and exhibitions, the museum houses the Southern Arts Craft Collection, which can be viewed by appointment. On the last Saturday of the month, between May and October, the balconied roof is open to the public. It was here that buns were thrown to celebrate the coronation of George III, beginning a tradition that is still upheld on royal occasions.

③ Keep ahead when the path merges with a wide track and, when it curves left by a pair of cottages, look for a stile on the right. Go diagonally across the field, briefly cutting through undergrowth into the next pasture. Keep quite close to the left boundary and aim for some tall trees and houses in the distance. Make for a footbridge in the top right-hand corner of the field. Walk ahead towards the outskirts of Abingdon and join a tarmac path. This is **Overmead**.

④ Turn right at the road and walk through the housing estate to the T-junction. Turn left and keep alongside the Thames to the **Old Anchor Inn**. Pass the pub and then turn left by some almshouses. Keep the **Church of St Helen** on the right

and head for the road. Cross over into **East St Helen Street** and make for the Old County Hall.

**WHERE TO EAT AND DRINK**
Abingdon has a variety of pubs from which to choose. The **Old Anchor** has a range of home-cooked food and a patio garden, while the **Broad Face** menu includes baguettes, jacket potatoes, toasties, ploughman's lunches, chicken Kiev and ham, egg and chips. The **George and Dragon** at Sutton Courtenay is a well-established village pub.

⑤ Turn right to reach **Bridge Street**, pass the **Broad Face** pub and cross the **River Thames** to the far bank. Go down the steps on the left to the tow path, pass under the road bridge and walk along the riverside path. Pass an illustrated map of Abingdon, go through a gate and cross meadows alongside the Thames, passing the ancient **Culham Bridge** on the left. Follow the line of **Culham Reach** and keep beside the water until you reach a sign for Sutton Courtenay.

⑥ Once over the cut follow the path across fields and back to the Thames. Cross several bridges and weirs at **Sutton Pools** and keep ahead at the road, passing **The Wharf** on the right. Follow the village street to the parish church and return to the car park.

**WHAT TO LOOK FOR**
The 12th to 14th century **church** at Sutton Courtenay is well worth a look. Herbert Asquith (1852–1928), British Liberal Prime Minister between 1908 and 1916, is buried in the churchyard, as is Eric Blair (1903–50), better known as George Orwell who, of course, wrote *Animal Farm* and *Nineteen Eighty-Four*. Blair took his pseudonym from the River Orwell in Suffolk.

# Around the Lakes of the Cotswold Water Park

*Through an evolving landscape in the southern Cotswolds.*

**Walk 24**

| | |
|---|---|
| **•DISTANCE•** | 5 miles (8km) |
| **•MINIMUM TIME•** | 2hrs |
| **•ASCENT / GRADIENT•** | Negligible ▲▲▲ |
| **•LEVEL OF DIFFICULTY•** | 🚶 🚶 🚶 |
| **•PATHS•** | Track, tow path and lanes, 10 stiles |
| **•LANDSCAPE•** | Dead flat – lakes, light woodland, canal and village |
| **•SUGGESTED MAP•** | aqua3 OS Explorer 169 Cirencester & Swindon |
| **•START / FINISH•** | Grid reference: SU 048974 |
| **•DOG FRIENDLINESS•** | Good but be aware of a lot of waterfowl around lakes |
| **•PARKING•** | Silver Street, South Cerney |
| **•PUBLIC TOILETS•** | None on route |

## BACKGROUND TO THE WALK

By their very nature, ancient landscapes and historic architecture evolve very slowly, changing little from one century to another. Can they resist the demands of a brasher era? In the Cotswolds the answer to this question is essentially 'yes'. Here building restrictions are strict – even, sometimes, draconian. The result, however, is a significant area of largely unspoilt English countryside; sometimes, thoughtful development has even enhanced an otherwise lacklustre skyline. The Cotswold Water Park, located in and around old gravel pits, is an example of this.

### Recreational Gravel

Gravel has been worked in the upper Thames Valley, where the water table is close to the surface, since the 1920s. The removal of gravel leads to the creation of lakes and in the areas around South Cerney and between Fairford and Lechlade there are now some 4,000 acres (1,620ha) of water, in about 100 lakes. They provide an important wetland habitat for a variety of wildlife. Most of these lakes have been turned over to recreational use of one sort or another, being a perfect place for game and coarse fishing, board sailing, walking, boating of various kinds, riding and sundry other leisure activities. Interestingly, this has been what is now called a private/public enterprise. The landscaping has not just been a case of letting nature take over where the gravel excavators left off. The crane-grabs that were used for excavation in the 1960s, for example, left the gravel pits with vertical sides and therefore with deep water right up to the shoreline. As it happens, some forms of aquatic life flourish under these conditions, but in other lakes the shoreline has been graded to create a gentler slope, to harmonise better with the flat landscape in this part of the Cotswolds and to suit the needs of swimmers and children. In the same way, trees have been planted and hills have been constructed to offer shelter and visual relief. Old brick railway bridges have been preserved. Finally, a style of waterside architecture has been developed to attract people to live here. It continues to evolve, just as the surrounding countryside has done for centuries.

**Walk 24**

### South Cerney and Cerney Wick

The walk begins in South Cerney, by the River Churn, only 4 miles (6.4km) from the source of the Thames. Look inside the Norman church for the exceptional carving on the 12th-century rood. Later the walk takes you through Cerney Wick, a smaller village on the other side of the gravel workings. The highlight here is an 18th-century roundhouse, used by the workers on the now disused Thames and Severn Canal.

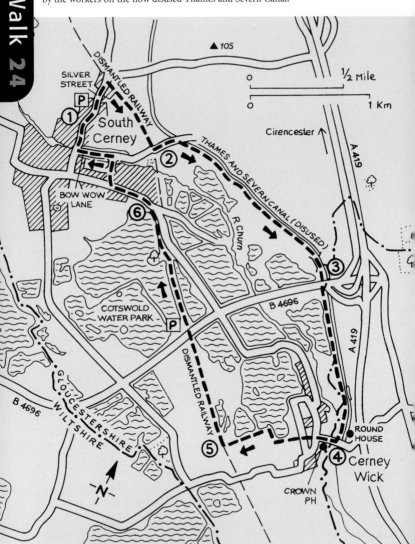

## Walk 24 **Directions**

① From **Silver Street** walk north out of the village. Immediately before the turning to Driffield and

Cricklade, turn right over a stile on to a bank. Stay on this obvious path for 800yds (732m), to reach a brick bridge across the path. Turn right here up a flight of steps to reach a narrow road.

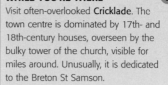

**Walk 24**

② Turn left and walk along here for 200yds (183m) until you come to footpaths to the right and left. Turn right along a farm track, following a signpost for **Cerney Wick**. Almost immediately the shallow, overgrown remains of the **Thames and Severn Canal** appear to your left. When the track veers right into a farm, walk ahead over a stile to follow a path beneath the trees – the old canal tow path. At a bridge keep ahead across stiles and continue until you come to a busy road.

---

**WHILE YOU'RE THERE** ⓘ
Visit often-overlooked **Cricklade**. The town centre is dominated by 17th- and 18th-century houses, overseen by the bulky tower of the church, visible for miles around. Unusually, it is dedicated to the Breton St Samson.

---

**WHERE TO EAT AND DRINK** ⓘ
The walk passes the **Crown** in Cerney Wick. There are also several pubs in South Cerney – the **Old George** and the **Eliot Arms** in Clarks Hay, and the **Royal Oak** on the High Street.

---

③ Cross with care. On the far side you have two choices: either continue on the tow path or take the path that skirts the lakes. If you take the lakeside path, you will eventually be able to rejoin the tow path by going left at a bridge after 600yds (549m). Continue until, after just under ½ mile (800m), you pass an old canal roundhouse across the canal to the left and, soon after, reach a lane at **Cerney Wick**.

④ Turn right here and walk to the junction at the end of the road, beside the **Crown** pub. Cross to a stile and enter a field. Walk straight ahead and come to another stile. Cross this aiming to the left of a cottage. Cross the lane, go over another stile and enter a field. Walk ahead and follow the path as it guides you across a stile on to the grass by a lake. Walk around the lake, going right and then left. In the corner before you, cross into a field, walk ahead towards trees and cross a stile to a track.

⑤ Turn right, rejoining the **old railway line** and following it all the way to a road. Cross this into a car park and go through a gate on to a track. Stay on this all the way to another road and follow a path that runs to its left.

⑥ Where the path ends at the beginning of **South Cerney**, continue along **Station Road**. Ignore a footpath on the right but turn right at the second one, which takes you across a bridge and brings you to a lane called '**Bow Wow**'. Turn left here between streams and return to **Silver Street**.

---

**WHAT TO LOOK FOR** ⓘ
Disused **transport systems** feature greatly in this walk. For much of it you will be beside or close to the old Thames and Severn Canal, or following the route of the old Andoversford railway line. The line linked Cheltenham and Swindon between 1891 and 1961. The **roundhouse** seen on the far side of the old canal as you approach Cerney Wick was used by lock keepers and maintenance engineers. This design was a distinctive feature of the Thames and Severn Canal. Even the windows were rounded to afford the occupants maximum visibility of their stretch of canal. The downstairs would have been used as a stable, the middle storey as a living area and the upstairs held sleeping accommodation. The flat roof was also put to use collecting rainwater for the house's water supply.

**Walk 25**

# Two Faces of the Haven

*The waters of Milford Haven and the coastline that forms its entrance.*

| | |
|---|---|
| **•DISTANCE•** | 8 miles (12.9km) |
| **•MINIMUM TIME•** | 3hrs 30min |
| **•ASCENT / GRADIENT•** | 1,017ft (310m) ▲▲▲ |
| **•LEVEL OF DIFFICULTY•** | 🚶 🚶 🚶 |
| **•PATHS•** | Coast path and easy tracks over agricultural land, short road section, 37 stiles |
| **•LANDSCAPE•** | Rugged coastline, magnificent beach and sheltered harbour |
| **•SUGGESTED MAP•** | aqua3 OS Explorer OL36 South Pembrokeshire |
| **•START / FINISH•** | Grid reference: SM 854031 |
| **•DOG FRIENDLINESS•** | Care needed near livestock |
| **•PARKING•** | Car park at West Angle Bay |
| **•PUBLIC TOILETS•** | At start and just off route in Angle village |

## BACKGROUND TO THE WALK

The narrow finger of land that juts out between Freshwater West and Angle Bay forms the eastern wall of the mouth of Milford Haven. On the northern edge of the peninsula, the waters are passive, lapping against a coastline that's gentle and sloping, but as you round the headland, a radical transformation takes place. Here, the cliffs stand tall and proud, defiantly resisting the full brunt of the considerable Atlantic swells. There are other differences too. While the views along the seaward coast are wild and unspoilt, the inner shores of the Haven reveal the ugly scars of industry. The smoking chimneys of the oil refinery dominate the eastern skyline and the inshore waters are criss-crossed with an unsightly patchwork of jetties.

### Challenging Route
The narrow-necked shape of the peninsula lends itself to a challenging circular walk that shows both sides of the coin. The outward leg, as far as the sweeping sands of Freshwater West, is about as tough as coast path walking gets; constantly dipping and climbing on narrow, often quite exposed, paths. The return leg is a little more civilised, tracking easily around the curve of Angle Bay and following field edges back out on to the headland.

### Whaling Town
Milford Haven is the name of both a huge natural inlet, once described by Admiral Nelson as 'the finest port in Christendom', and the small town that nestles on its northern shores. Despite the obvious advantages of the sheltered waterways, the Haven saw only limited development until the 20th century. Although there is evidence of earlier settlements and shipping activity, the town, as it is now, and original dock, sprang up in the late 1700s to house a small whaling community that had fled from Nantucket, Massachusetts, during the American War of Independence. Despite interest from the military, which saw the potential for shipbuilding, lack of funding at the time prohibited serious expansion. Various enterprising ideas followed over the ensuing years, but by the end of the 19th century, the whaling had all but declined and the Navy had moved to nearby Pembroke Dock.

## Lifelines and Controversy

Large-scale fishing in the rich waters of the Pembrokeshire coast threw the port a lifeline in the early 1900s and then, as this too declined, mainly due to over-fishing and the related smaller catches, energy production took over as the area's main industry. There were once three refineries and a power station at the head of the Haven. One of the refineries has now closed and the power station is being dismantled after bowing to considerable public pressure against its plan to burn Orimulsion, a controversial fuel with a contested safety record, instead of oil.

**Walk 25**

# Walk 25 Directions

① Facing the sea, walk left out of the car park and pass between the café and the public conveniences to a waymarked stile. Follow the field edge along, crossing further stiles to a narrow, hedged track that leads to a set of stone steps.

② Follow a good track for a few paces and then fork right to drop towards the ruined **tower** on the headland. Continue back up, cross more stiles and then go down to a footbridge. Climb up from this and pass **Sheep Island** on your right.

---

**WHAT TO LOOK FOR**

Milford Haven's potential vulnerability to invasion has led to considerable defences being constructed around its entrance. The stone **blockhouse** on Thorn Island, now a hotel, is testament to this, as are the other fortifications on St Ann's Head.

---

③ Continue along the coast, dropping steeply into a succession of valleys and climbing back up each time. As you reach the northern end of **Freshwater West**, keep your eye open for a footpath waymarker to the left.

④ Cross a stile and walk up the floor of the valley, swinging left to a stile at the top. Cross the next field, and another stile, and continue to the road (**B4320**). Turn left on to the road and walk past a cluster of houses to a right-hand turn. Follow this down to the coast, turn left on to the coast path and merge on to a drive.

⑤ Take the drive to a footpath sign on the right. If the tide is low, you can cross the estuary here and continue along the bank of pebbles to the road on the other side. If it's not, carry on along the road into **Angle** village and bear right by the church to follow a dirt track along the other side.

---

**WHILE YOU'RE THERE**

Take a drive or, better still, a walk across the magnificent **Cleddau toll bridge** that spans the estuary between Neyland and Pembroke Dock. The sweeping curve of the lofty 1970s construction provides stunning views over the whole haven and the coast beyond. It also makes the best connection between North and South Pembrokeshire. To get there follow the A477 from Pembroke.

---

⑥ Continue around, pass the **Old Point House Inn** on your left and follow field edges to the gravel turning point above the **lifeboat station** on your right. Keep straight ahead, over a stile, and follow the bottom of the field system into a wooded area.

⑦ You'll join a broad track that runs around **Chapel Bay cottages** and fort. Keep right, to cross a stile and follow the narrow path back above the coast. This rounds the headland by **Thorn Island**.

⑧ As you descend into **West Angle Bay**, the path diverts briefly into a field to avoid a landslide. Continue downwards and bear right on to a drive that drops you back to the car park.

---

**WHERE TO EAT AND DRINK**

The **Hibernia Inn** in Angle village is conveniently placed for lunch or a drink, but there's also the **Wavecrest Café**, at the start of the walk, and the stunningly positioned **Old Point House Inn**, as you climb above Angle Bay and back out on to the headland.

# A Rocky Ramble Around the Head

*An easy stroll around the dramatic cliffs of one of mainland Britain's most westerly points.*

**Walk 26**

| | |
|---:|:---|
| **·DISTANCE·** | 3½ miles (5.7km) |
| **·MINIMUM TIME·** | 2hrs |
| **·ASCENT / GRADIENT·** | 425ft (130m) ▲▲ ▲ ▲ |
| **·LEVEL OF DIFFICULTY·** | 🚶🚶 🚶🚶 🚶🚶 |
| **·PATHS·** | Coast path, clear paths across heathland, 2 stiles |
| **·LANDSCAPE·** | Dramatic cliffs, heather- and gorse-covered hillsides |
| **·SUGGESTED MAP·** | aqua3 OS Explorer OL35 North Pembrokeshire |
| **·START / FINISH·** | Grid reference: SM 734271 |
| **·DOG FRIENDLINESS·** | Care needed near livestock |
| **·PARKING·** | Whitesands Beach |
| **·PUBLIC TOILETS·** | At start |

## BACKGROUND TO THE WALK

Steeped in legend, peppered with the evidence of civilisations past, and scenically stunning, it would be difficult to imagine a more atmospheric place than St David's Head. For full effect, visit at sunset and watch the sky turn red over the scattered islets of the Bishops and Clerks.

### St David's Head

Carn Llidi, a towering monolith of ancient rock that has all the attributes of a full blown mountain, yet stands only 594ft (181m) above sea level, dominates the headland. Its heather- and gorse-covered flanks are alive with small heathland birds, which chatter from the swaying ferns and dart for cover in the hidden crannies of dry-stone walls.

The coast, when you meet it, is at its intricate finest; a succession of narrow zawns (clefts), broken up by stubborn headlands that thrust defiantly into the ever present swells. The Head itself is magnificent and a few minutes spent exploring will quickly uncover a series of rocky terraces that offer shelter from the wind and stunning views over the ocean to Ramsey Island and the Bishops and Clerks.

### The Warrior's Dyke

Despite its hostile demeanour, St David's Head was once home to a thriving Iron-Age community who lived in huts and kept their stock in a field system, the remains of which are still visible. The headland, naturally guarded by the ocean on three sides, was also defended by the Clawdd-y-Milwry (the Warrior's Dyke) at its eastern edge. The dyke is actually formed by three ditches and two ramparts that cut across the neck of the headland. The main bastion, a dry-stone wall that would have once stood around 15ft (4.6m) tall, is still easily visible as a linear pile of stones and rocks. Within the fort there are a number of standing stones, stone circles and the remains of basic huts. The defences are thought to have been built around AD 100.

Walk 26

### Burial Chambers

At least 3,000 years older, but well worth seeking out, is Coetan Arthur, a neolithic quoit, or burial chamber, which stands directly above a narrow zawn, bounded on its eastern walls by the red-coloured crags of Craig Coetan, a popular climbing venue. Coetan Arthur consists of a 12ft (3.7m) long capstone, propped up on a smaller rock. The quoit would have originally been covered with earth to form a mound, but this has long since been eroded away. There is evidence of several more burial chambers near the summit of Carn Llidi. Happily both the headland and Carn Llidi are in the care of the National Trust, and you are free to wander at will to investigate these fascinating sites, although you should bear in mind that they are Scheduled Ancient Monuments and protected by law.

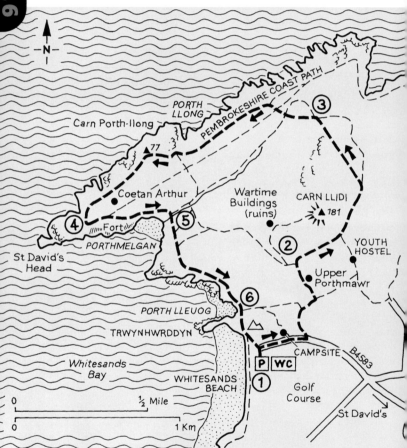

## Walk 26 Directions

① From **Whitesands Beach** head back up the road, pass the **campsite**, and a track on the left, and then take the second track on the left. Bear right where it splits and continue around a left-hand bend to walk up to the buildings. Keep left to walk between the houses, then carry on to a gate.

② Turn right on to the open heathland and follow the footpath along the wall beneath **Carn Llidi**.

Walk 26

Pass the track that drops to the youth hostel on the right and continue around to where the path splits. Take the higher track and keep going in the same direction until, at the corner of a wall, a clear track runs diagonally left towards the coast.

③ Follow this to the coast path and turn left to hug the cliff tops. At **Porth Llong**, the path bears right to climb to a cairn. The headland is a labyrinth of paths and tracks, but for maximum enjoyment try to stick as close to the cliff tops as possible as you round a number of narrow zawns. The official coast path doesn't go as far as the tip of the peninsula, but plenty of other tracks do, so follow one as far as you wish.

④ From the tip, turn left and make your way through the rocky outcrops on the southern side of the headland. As you approach **Porthmelgan** you'll pick up an obvious path that traverses the steep hillside down into a valley, which shelters a small stream.

⑤ Cross the stream and climb up the steps on the other side. Continue to a kissing gate where the National Trust land ends and maintain your direction. Pass above **Porth Lleuog** and the distinctive rocky promontory of **Trwynhwrddyn**, which is worth a visit in its own right.

⑥ The path then drops steeply down to the road at the entrance to **Whitesands Beach**.

Walk 27

# Ombersley and Holt Fleet

*Explore an estate park and the banks of the River Severn.*

| | |
|---|---|
| **•DISTANCE•** | 5¾ miles (9.2km) |
| **•MINIMUM TIME•** | 2hrs 30min |
| **•ASCENT / GRADIENT•** | 200ft (61m) |
| **•LEVEL OF DIFFICULTY•** | |
| **•PATHS•** | Riverside paths, field paths and tracks, village street, 9 stiles |
| **•LANDSCAPE•** | Estate parkland, riverside meadows and general farmland |
| **•SUGGESTED MAP•** | aqua3 OS Explorer 204 Worcester & Droitwich Spa |
| **•START / FINISH•** | Grid reference: SO 845630 |
| **•DOG FRIENDLINESS•** | Few off-lead opportunities unless very obedient |
| **•PARKING•** | Towards southern end of road through Ombersley on eastern side (southbound exit from village) |
| **•PUBLIC TOILETS•** | None on route |

## BACKGROUND TO THE WALK

Ombersley must have been awful before the bypass, but now it verges on the tranquil. Ombersley Court was built in the 1720s. Apparently it has a superb interior, but the nearest you'll get to even a reasonable view of it is at the far end of the churchyard (beside a grim memorial tree). Sited on the Ombersley Park Estate, St Andrew's Church was built 100 years after Ombersley Court, but in the decorated style of the early 14th century, presumably to reflect the fragment of the original church (now a mausoleum) behind it.

### Silence of the Owls

Along the river towards Holt Bridge, to your right (and left also) is a classic stretch of woodland, adorning the steep slopes of the great River Severn's flood plain. If you were to walk along here at dusk you could hope to see an owl, possibly even a barn owl, but you probably wouldn't. A survey conducted in Worcestershire in 1932 found 184 breeding pairs of barn owls, but a similar survey in 1985 found just 32. There were numerous reasons for its decline. Part of the blame is apportioned to the grubbing out of the hedgerows, thereby removing a good habitat for small mammals. However, much is apportioned to intensive agriculture's use of pesticides, moving along the food chain so that, by the time a barn owl has eaten 100 or so slightly contaminated but well mammals (mice, shrews, voles), the cumulative dosage of pesticide is fatal.

The goal of the Worcestershire Barn Owl Society (WBOS) is to reverse the trend, partly by breeding barn owls and releasing them in carefully chosen locations. Barn owls are quite happy in tree hollows but, no, they rarely approve of barn conversions. The WBOS builds and erects nest boxes in strategic places to compensate for the loss – you can even buy or sponsor one. Like other owls, the barn owl flies silently, a useful hunting trick, achieved by having soft tips to its wing feathers – these tips effectively deaden any airflow noise.

### Holt Fleet

The bridge at Holt Fleet replaced a ferry. It was the last in Worcestershire to cease taking tolls. (In Herefordshire tolls are still taken at the 1802 Whitney Bridge.) Such was the belief in a German invasion that mines were laid under the Holt Fleet Bridge during the Second World War. The Holt Fleet Inn was built well before the bridge, and benefited greatly from the day-tripper business, being the northern terminus for paddle steamer trips from Worcester, about 7 miles (11.3km) to the south. These trips ran until the 1930s. In contrast, the Wharf Inn, on the east bank, marks the site of a coal wharf. Holt Lock, a little way upstream, was completed in 1844.

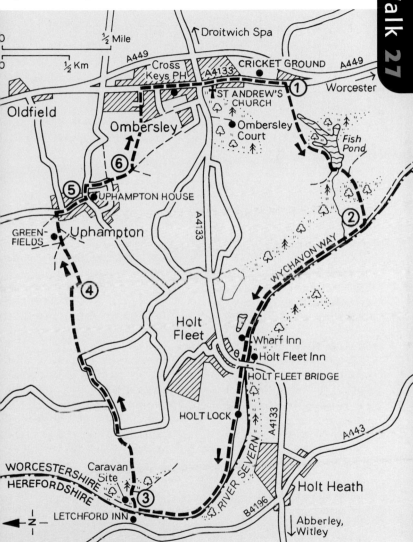

## Walk 27 Directions

① To the south of the village, and beyond the **cricket ground**, take a path on the right. This is the

**Wychavon Way**. Briefly in trees, walk across a meadow to a stile beside a willow. Go along the left-hand field edge, and briefly by the water's edge. At the corner of the fish pond a waymarker leads out to

**Walk 27**

a track. Turn left, following this track right in 80yds (73m). It becomes a sunken path through delicious woodland. Cross a meadow to the river.

② Turn right. In a short mile (1.6km) you'll pass two fishing pools to reach **Holt Fleet Bridge**. Go under this, continuing for about the same distance, passing the staffed **Holt Lock**. When opposite the **Letchford Inn** you'll come to a riverside stile.

③ Don't go over this stile; instead, turn right. In the field corner join the access road. At a junction go straight ahead on the public road. In 650yds (594m), at a right-hand bend, keep this line by moving left, on to a farm track. The large area on the right was formerly an orchard, but it has gone completely. It's over ¼ mile (400m) to the top of

this field. When you are 30yds (27m) before a rusty shed, turn right. Now, in about 75yds (69m), go left, over a stile.

④ What could be a golf course fairway turns out to be an enormous garden. Aim to pass to the right of the house, by a children's wooden watchtower. Cross the gravel in front of the house, **Greenfields**, to go down its private driveway. Turn right for 275yds (251m), passing several black-and-white houses, to a T-junction – **Uphampton House** is in front of you.

⑤ Turn left for 110yds (100m), then turn right, uphill. In 150yds (137m) don't bend right but go straight ahead, on a shingly track. About 220yds (201m) further, the main track bends right, a rough track goes ahead and a public footpath goes half left.

⑥ Take the public footpath option, along a field edge. Continue through a small area of market garden, reaching a cul-de-sac. Shortly turn right, along the village street. There are many houses to look at, the churches of St Andrew (current and former), and several points of refreshment to delay your return to your car.

# An Antiquary and Shustoke Reservoir

*A stroll around the reservoir and into Church End reveals changes in the landscape since Sir William Dugdale's days.*

| | |
|---|---|
| •DISTANCE• | 3½ miles (5.7km) |
| •MINIMUM TIME• | 1hr 15min |
| •ASCENT / GRADIENT• | 98ft (30m) ▲▲▲ |
| •LEVEL OF DIFFICULTY• | 🚶 🚶 🚶 |
| •PATHS• | Lakeside paths and field-edge footpaths, 11 stiles |
| •LANDSCAPE• | Reservoir parkland, farmland and residential areas |
| •SUGGESTED MAP• | aqua3 OS Explorer 232 Nuneaton & Tamworth |
| •START / FINISH• | Grid reference: SP 225910 |
| •DOG FRIENDLINESS• | Under control at all times |
| •PARKING• | Severn Trent car park, Shustoke |
| •PUBLIC TOILETS• | At car park |

## BACKGROUND TO THE WALK

The beautiful Shustoke Reservoir, together with nearby Whitacre Water Works, supplies water to the bulk storage reservoirs at Coventry and Nuneaton. The reservoir is a well-used sailing venue and is also popular with anglers and walkers.

### Ancient Scotscote

The small village of Shustoke, from which the reservoir takes its name, lies on the edge of Warwickshire. It's a large parish, some 2,000 acres (810ha), but much of this is now under water. The village was mentioned in the Domesday survey as Scotscote, but has gone through a series of name changes over the centuries including Schustoke, Sydestoke, Shestoke, Schristoke, Sheistock and Shstooke. It's origins perhaps lie in the Saxon 'sceat' meaning 'nook' or 'corner of land'. This was once a thriving agricultural community, but much of its old way of life disappeared with the social and economic changes which followed World War Two.

Shustoke's most famous son is undoubtedly Sir William Dugdale (1605–86), the author of *The Antiquities of Warwickshire*. He was born at the old rectory in Shawbury Lane, the son of a Lancashire gentleman who settled in Warwickshire after marrying late in life. Today a large part of the local land is still owned by the Dugdale family.

William Dugdale was schooled at Coventry, and came back to live at Blyth Hill in Shustoke after his marriage in 1625. He was one of a group of local gentry who took up the study of local history, and it was through this that he came into contact with members of the court of Charles I. He secured a post at the College of Arms, and spent most of the Civil War in the Royalist stronghold of Oxford, where he was able to pursue his studies in the Bodleian Library. As well as Warwickshire, he focused his attention on English monastic houses. The first volume of his *Monasticon Anglicacanum* was published in 1655, two more huge volumes following in 1661 and 1673. *The Antiquities of Warwickshire*, the most detailed study of its day, was published in 1655.

The Restoration was kind to Dugdale and he was able to continue with his heraldic work all over the country. He was appointed Garter King of Arms in 1677 and died, aged 80, in 1686. He was buried in the village.

**East and West**
Shustoke is a divided village because of an outbreak of the plague in 1650. It used to surround St Cuthbert's Church, but the houses were moved to the west to get away from the contaminated site. The church, with its barrel roof and slender spire, still stands proudly on a hilltop at the eastern end of the village. In the 19th century, a bolt of lightning almost destroyed the building, but it has survived and inside you can see a monument to Sir William Dugdale.

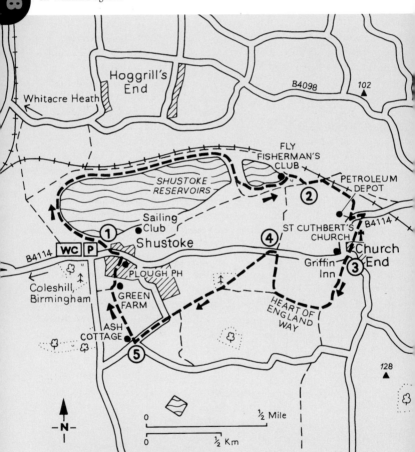

# Walk 28 **Directions**

① Leave the car park going past the public toilets and follow the fingerpost to the Circular Path which goes around the larger of the two **Shustoke reservoirs**. Steps lead on to the central strip of land where you turn right. At the end of the strip, bear left and continue along the wide path which is a short distance to the south of the smaller reservoir to protect you from the

**Walk 28**

---

### WHILE YOU'RE THERE ⓘ

Not far away from Shustoke is **Hoar Park Farm**, an 18th-century farm complex, which has been converted to accommodate a lively craft village and children's farm. There is also a country shopping area, an antiques centre, a garden centre and a restaurant, open all year round from Tuesday to Sunday.

### WHAT TO LOOK FOR ⓘ

Shustoke attracts a wide range of **birdlife** to its valuable open water. As well as pochard, teal, widgeon and tufted duck the occasional osprey has been sighted, dipping this way on its passage south in November. You may also spy the distinctive profile of a cormorant, patiently fishing at the water's edge.

---

possible danger of fly fishing lines. After passing behind the buildings of the **Fly Fisherman's Club**, leave the reservoir complex over a stile and continue ahead into woodland, with the railway line to your left.

② Emerge from the trees via a stile and walk along the field hedge up to the **B4114** at the entrance to a petroleum depot. Turn left along the road edge for 80yds (73m), then cross the road and go through a kissing gate into the pasture below **St Cuthbert's Church**. Walk up the field and go through a second kissing gate to the right-hand side of the churchyard and take the lane past the church to **Shawbury Lane**.

### WHERE TO EAT AND DRINK ⓘ

The **Plough**, by The Green, offers traditional ales, quality meals and bed and breakfast. It's popular with rambling groups and families (dogs in the bar only). The **Griffin Inn** at Church End has a good selection of bar snacks and serves Vicars Ruin ale. Children welcome in the conservatory, dogs in the bar area.

③ Cross the lane and then go over a stile, situated a little to the right, into the field opposite, following the direction of the waymarkers across two fields until you meet up with the **Heart of England Way**. Go right and follow the Way around the next two

fields to **Church Road**, then go left along it for 50yds (46m).

④ At the end of a small row of cottages, turn left again over a stile and take the public footpath through a small copse and then by the side of the hedge until you come to a farm track that leads to the corner of a lane. Continue ahead along the lane.

⑤ Just before you reach **Ash Cottage**, go right over a stile and follow the footpath across a cultivated field to a stile to the left of **Green Farm**. A final stile to the right of **Greenacre** (cottage) leads into a residential lane. Continue ahead and you will soon reach The Green in Shustoke, close to the **Plough** and at the side of the B4114 (**Coleshill Road**). Go left and then right into the Severn Trent car park.

# Draycote Water, Dunchurch and Thurlaston

*An easy walk around Warwickshire's largest reservoir and into two historic villages.*

| | |
|---|---|
| **•DISTANCE•** | 6½ miles (10.4km) |
| **•MINIMUM TIME•** | 2hrs |
| **•ASCENT / GRADIENT•** | 164ft (50m) ▲ ▲ ▲ |
| **•LEVEL OF DIFFICULTY•** | 🚶 🚶 🚶 |
| **•PATHS•** | Reservoir paths and field paths, 7 stiles |
| **•LANDSCAPE•** | Reservoir in gentle rolling countryside |
| **•SUGGESTED MAP•** | aqua3 OS Explorer 222 Rugby & Daventry |
| **•START / FINISH•** | Grid reference: SP 462690 |
| **•DOG FRIENDLINESS•** | On lead at all times |
| **•PARKING•** | Pay-and-display car park at Draycote Water |
| **•PUBLIC TOILETS•** | At country park |

## BACKGROUND TO THE WALK

This walk offers the opportunity to explore the largest area of open water in Warwickshire and to visit two nearby historic villages. The impressive Draycote Water reservoir is set in more than 600 acres (243ha) of land and attracts large numbers of wildfowl. Owned by Severn Trent Water, it was completed in 1970 as a pumped storage facility. It's refilled during winter months from the nearby River Leam, thus reducing the risk of local flooding. There is a fine retrospective view of Draycote Water on your way to lovely Dunchurch village.

### Gunpowder Plot and Treason

A private house in Dunchurch is now called Guy Fawkes but was formerly the Falcon Inn. It was here that the gunpowder plot conspirators sought refuge from justice in 1605, after their failed attempt to assassinate King James I as he visited parliament. Dunchurch was once a busy coaching village and the Dun Cow is the old coaching inn, conveniently situated at the village crossroads. The historical perspective continues on the village green, where you will see the old stocks and an ancient cross. By the crossroads is a statue commemorating Lord John Scott, a local landowner and sportsman who, at the time of his death, had recently equipped a new boat to investigate some of the problems of deep-sea fishing.

The 14th-century St Peter's Church has a fine tower, a Norman door and a Norman font. Set inside folding doors is a monument to Thomas Newcombe who was 'a printer to three kings' and founded the 17th-century almshouses. These now add an air of old world charm to the hotchpotch of thatched properties in this pleasant village, which is full of floral colour in the spring and summer.

There is another fine view over the reservoir as you descend into the next village – Thurlaston. Again, a number of attractive thatched cottages will catch your eye as you enter, and you pass near to a sail-less windmill (now converted into a private residence). One intriguing road name here is Pudding Bag Lane. The Church of St Edmund was completed in 1848, originally to house the village school. The site was donated by Lord John Scott (he of the statue by the crossroads). The building was used as a church on Sundays, but accommodation for the schoolmaster was built into the tower. The present bell tower was added later, but the schoolmaster's accommodation remains as a private residence. Bizarrely the bell rope still passes through one of its rooms. Returning to the car park, you will have completed a circuit of this wonderful reservoir.

Walk 29

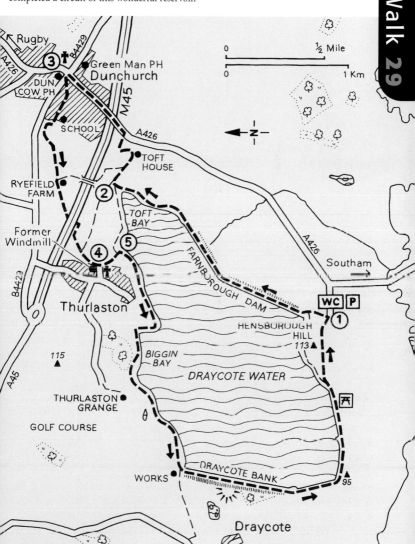

# Walk 29 Directions

① From Draycote Water car park proceed up to the reservoir and then bear right following the tarmac lane along the top of **Farnborough Dam** wall to reach **Toft Bay**.

② At the end of Toft Bay go right and leave the reservoir grounds via a handgate. Continue ahead and then go right and follow the waymarker signs to a footpath that climbs past llama pens up towards **Toft House**. Continue ahead along the hedged footpath to the left of the house. This bends left on to a lane where you go right up to the **A426** Rugby to Dunchurch road. Go left along the road, cross the road bridge and enter the village of **Dunchurch**, passing a number of attractive thatched properties. The **Village Square** and St Peter's Church are to the right of the crossroads, with the **Dun Cow**, an old coaching inn full of character, immediately opposite.

---

### WHILE YOU'RE THERE

Explore **Dunchurch** village. It once had some 27 alehouses but now has only two pubs. The stocks remain, but sadly the old gaol was pulled down in 1972, perhaps because there was no longer so much drinking taking place. The last person to be held in the gaol was a Peter Murcott who spent his night there supping ale through a straw from a barrel outside the window.

---

③ At the crossroads, go left along the pavement of the **B4429** past the Dunchurch & Thurlaston WMC. Bear left along **School Street** and follow the footpath past more thatched properties and the infant school down to the Dunchurch Scout Group Hall. Here, go right and then left along a footpath to the right of the playing fields. Continue along the hedged path and proceed to the right of **Ryefield Farm**. Go ahead over pastureland, then pass beneath the **M45** road bridge before diagonally crossing the next field to a pair of stiles to enter the village of **Thurlaston**.

④ Go to the left by **St Edmund's Church** and down a concrete farm track to a handgate and a footbridge to enter the perimeter of **Draycote Water**.

⑤ Go right along the walkway by the side of the reservoir around **Biggin Bay**. To your right **Thurlaston Grange** can be seen and then you will pass a golf course. Continue around the end of the reservoir, passing by the treatment works, and then stroll along **Draycote Bank**. To your right is the spire of Bourton-on-Dunsmore church about a mile (1.6km) away; to its right is Bourton Hall. After passing by a picnic area and just before reaching the yachting area go right on a footpath that leads up on to **Hensborough Hill** for a fine view of the surrounding area. Meander past the trig point, some 371ft (113m) above sea level, and return to the car park.

---

### WHERE TO EAT AND DRINK

There are a couple of pubs in Dunchurch. The **Green Man** is situated along the B4429 Daventry Road. The **Dun Cow** at the crossroads in the centre of the village is a popular eating place for local walkers and welcomes children but not dogs (except guide dogs).

---

### WHAT TO LOOK FOR

St Peter's Church and **Bourton Hall** are local landmarks to the west of Draycote Water and are clearly visible as you walk around the beautiful reservoir. Situated on Dunsmore Heath in the village of Bourton-on-Dunsmore, St Peter's has a fine 13th-century font, a Jacobean altar and a ghost in its vestry. The 18th-century Bourton Hall, restored in 1979, is a manor house which can date its establishment all the way back to a Saxon by the name of Lewin.

# A Rutland Waterside Walk

*A short but scenic introduction to the aquatic charms of Rutland Water.*

| | |
|---|---|
| •DISTANCE• | 4½ miles (7.2km) |
| •MINIMUM TIME• | 2hrs 30min |
| •ASCENT / GRADIENT• | 311ft (95m) ▲ ▲ ▲ |
| •LEVEL OF DIFFICULTY• | 朮 朮 朮 |
| •PATHS• | Wide and firm the whole distance |
| •LANDSCAPE• | Low-lying peninsula of dipping fields and woodland |
| •SUGGESTED MAP• | aqua3 OS Explorer 234 Rutland Water |
| •START / FINISH• | Grid reference: SK 900075 |
| •DOG FRIENDLINESS• | On lead in fields of stock and around nesting birds |
| •PARKING• | Roadside parking in Upper Hambleton |
| •PUBLIC TOILETS• | None on route (nearest in Oakham) |

## BACKGROUND TO THE WALK

That England's smallest county contains its biggest stretch of inland water is impressive enough, but in fact Rutland Water's 3,100 acres (1,255ha) make it one of the largest artificial lakes in the whole of western Europe.

Work began in 1973 with the flooding of the Gwash Valley and abandonment of the two villages of Nether and Middle Hambleton, but Anglia Water's reservoir is about much more than simply the supply of drinking water. Sailing and windsurfing are very popular, while fishermen are to be found on the shores and out in boats in virtually all weathers. There are picnic sites along the northern edge, a museum at the preserved church at Normanton on the southern shore, and afternoon cruises on the *Rutland Belle* that plies the water daily between May and September. A 25-mile (40km) off-road cycling route encompasses the whole of Rutland Water, and cycle hire is available at Whitwell and Normanton in the summer months.

### An Ornithological Feast

The nature reserve at the far western end of Rutland Water is managed by Leicestershire and Rutland Wildlife Trust, and your first port of call should be the Anglian Water Birdwatching Centre at Egleton. From here you can obtain a permit to walk to the 15 different hides that dot the secluded bays and artificially created lagoons, or go on to visit Lyndon Nature Reserve on the southern side of Manton Bay. Rutland Water is one of the most important centres for wildfowl in Britain – as many as 23,500 ducks have been recorded on a single winter's day, and a total of 250 different species of birds have been seen since 1975.

Ducks such as pochard, teal, gadwall and shoveler are a common sight, while waders like redshank and sandpipers are frequent visitors. An hour or two in a hide and your list will probably include terns, lapwing, cormorants, grebes, and so on, plus perhaps a more unusual sighting such as merganser or godwit.

However, there is one rare fish-eating bird that has had the twitchers fumbling at their binocular cases over the past few years. In 1996 a programme was initiated to translocate young osprey chicks from Scotland to Rutland, and since then several of these majestic birds of prey have returned from their hazardous African migration to set up home at

Rutland – the first time ospreys have nested in England in over 150 years. However, the long-term fate of the Rutland ospreys is far from secure, since the birds mate for life and have very few chicks, but with careful protection and gentle encouragement the outlook for the so-called fish eagles is hopeful. The birds are generally present throughout the summer months and, although visible from hides, there is also a CCTV camera that relays close-up pictures of the birds back to the visitor centre at Egleton.

## Walk 30 Directions

① From **St Andrew's Church** in the centre of Upper Hambleton, walk eastwards on the long and level main street as far as the red pillar box. Turn left through the gate for the grassy lane indicated 'public footpath' that leads straight through a gate and down the middle of a sloping field.

② Go through the gate at the bottom and turn right on to the wide track that runs just above the shore. This popular and peaceful route around the Hambleton peninsula is also shared by cyclists, so enjoy the walk but be alert. Follow it from field to field, and through **Armley Wood**, with ever-changing views across Rutland Water. As you gradually swing around the tip of the Hambleton

Walk 30

peninsula with views towards the dam at the eastern end, you can begin to appreciate the sheer size of the reservoir, and how the birds, anglers, sailors and other users can all happily co-exist.

③ When you arrive at a tarmac lane (which is gated to traffic at this point, since it simply disappears into the water a little further on!), go straight across to continue on the same unmade track. It turns right and runs parallel with the road a short distance, before heading left and back towards the peaceful water's edge and a lovely section of mixed woodland.

*WHERE TO EAT AND DRINK* ℹ
The **Finch's Arms** at Upper Hambleton is an elegant public house where the emphasis is on high-quality bar food and restaurant meals, and from the back terrace there are great views out across the northern sweep of Rutland Water. Booking is advisable for peak times. A full range of cafés and pubs is to be found in **Oakham**, 3 miles (4.8km) away.

④ Approaching **Old Hall**, a handsome building perched just above the shore, turn left to reach its surfaced drive, then go right and walk along it for 160yds (146m) to reach a cattle grid.

*WHILE YOU'RE THERE* ℹ
Just to the south of Rutland Water is the picturesque village of Wing, where apart from two decent pubs there is a most unusual and historic maze. Cut into the roadside turf near the recreation ground, **Wing Maze** is based on an 11-ringed design often found on the floors of medieval French cathedrals. Wing itself once had a monastery, and it's possible that the monks may have followed the lines of the maze, stopping to pray at certain points.

*WHILE YOU'RE THERE* ℹ
It's said that there's no higher land between Upper Hambleton and the Wash and, although modest in height, the hilltop position of the village of course spared it from the watery fate that claimed its neighbours. Among the views from the peninsula is **Burley on the Hill**, a striking mansion on a densely wooded ridge to the north that was built for David Finch, Earl of Nottingham, between 1694 and 1705.

⑤ At this point you can return directly to **Upper Hambleton** by following the lane back uphill; otherwise veer left to continue along the open, waterside track, with views across to Egleton Bay and the corner of Rutland Water specially reserved for wildlife (it's out of bounds to sailing boats).

⑥ After about 500yds (457m) look for the easily missed stile in the hedge on your right, and the public footpath that heads straight up the field. (If you overshoot, or want to extend the walk by ½ mile (800m), simply carry on along the track to the very far end and return along the lane to the village.) Aim for the apex of the field, where successive stiles lead to a narrow passageway between a hedge and a fence that eventually brings you out in the churchyard in the centre of the village.

# Boats, Broads and Bulrushes

*Head-high reeds rustle all around as you walk from Loddon between the River Chet and Hardley Flood.*

| | |
|---|---|
| •DISTANCE• | 5¼ miles (8.4km) |
| •MINIMUM TIME• | 2hr 15min |
| •ASCENT / GRADIENT• | 98ft (30m) ▲▲▲ |
| •LEVEL OF DIFFICULTY• | 🚶🚶 🚶🚶 🚶🚶 |
| •PATHS• | Footpaths along waterways, farm tracks, paved roads, stiles, wading required where Hardley Flood meets River Chet |
| •LANDSCAPE• | Reed-fringed riverside and lakeside, farmland |
| •SUGGESTED MAP• | aqua3 OS Explorer OL40 The Broads |
| •START / FINISH• | Grid reference: TM 362986 |
| •DOG FRIENDLINESS• | On leads, especially around Hardley Flood nature reserve |
| •PARKING• | Free car park on Church Plain in Loddon (opposite Holy Trinity Church); or car park near river |
| •PUBLIC TOILETS• | At Loddon car park near river |

## BACKGROUND TO THE WALK

If you are interested in hidden gems of architecture then Loddon is the place for you, with buildings ranging from a medieval church to some of the largest council houses built to house the London overspill after the Second World War. Handsome Holy Trinity Church, on Church Plain, dates from the end of the 15th century – the height of Gothic Perpendicular – and is beautifully light and airy. Its showpiece is the two-storey porch with a spiral staircase and gorgeous carvings.

The library, dating from the mid-19th century, was originally a school and was converted to its present use in the 1970s. Attractive 17th- and 18th-century houses line the High Street, including one curiously called The Institute. Loddon House is perhaps the most ambitious building. It dates from 1711 and has five bays and a glorious collection of columns. It is not to be confused with Loddon Hall, which is located a mile (1.6km) to the south east of the village.

### Charming Council Homes

When Loddon became one of the many towns designated for new housing estates to help solve the post-war accommodation crisis, the Lowestoft architects Herbert Taylor and David Green were commissioned to design single-storey old peoples' homes. Those built in Davy Place are quite charming and the 78 homes in Hobart Road, Crossway Terrace and Drury Lane are spacious and of interest. The architects of many other council estates have not been so sensitive, and maybe they should visit Loddon to see that council guidelines and limited finances need not always produce dull results.

Loddon is famous for its watermill. This glorious building spans the River Chet and comprises a weather-boarded mill – dating mostly from the 18th-century, although parts are older – with an early 19th-century house attached to it. It is not open to the public.

This walk takes you through some of Norfolk's most attractive countryside, giving a taste of the silent and mysterious Broads and peaceful farmland, as well as sampling the delights of watching the boats jostle and jangle on their moorings along the banks of the busy River Chet. If you have time to spare, then you can stop for a while at the picnic site, where you can watch novice boatmen steering their crafts nervously towards the wider waterways of the Broads. Collisions are not unknown, and river watching can be both a relaxing and amusing pastime.

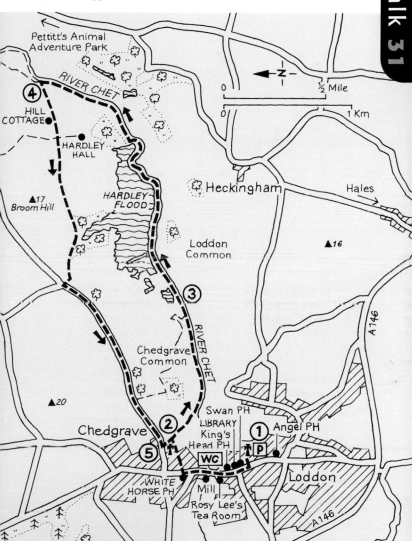

# Walk 31 Directions

① Turn right past the library on to **Bridge Street** and walk down the hill to cross the river into Chedgrave. At the **White Horse** go right, then start looking for the public footpath sign on your right just after the row of terraced houses. Meet a residential street, cross it to the footpath opposite, that runs between hedges, and continue to **Chedgrave church**.

② Turn right at the end of the graveyard, passing a meadow on your left before going through a small gate at the public footpath sign on your right. Nettles can grow in abundance here. Go through a second small gate that takes you on the path along the north bank of the **River Chet**. Cross two wooden footbridges, pass a sign telling you that this area is in the care of the Norfolk Wildlife Trust, and continue to a stile.

**WHERE TO EAT AND DRINK** ⓘ
Both the **Angel** and the **Swan** in Loddon serve good food, as does the **White Horse** over the river in Chedgrave. Loddon's **King's Head** (morning coffee, lunches and evening meals) is near the police station, and **Rosy Lee's Tea Room** is near the bridge. Loddon also offers a variety of take-aways, plus several general stores should you fancy a picnic (there is a picnic site on the Chet in Chedgrave).

③ Cross the stile and continue along the river path. Depending on the growth of reeds you may be able to see that you are on a causeway here, with the Chet on your right and the meres that comprise **Hardley Flood** on your left. Cross a second stile, after which you gain tantalising glimpses of the glittering waters of Hardley Flood and its abundant birdlife. It is well worth pausing here if you are interested in birdwatching, since the Trust has erected nesting areas in the water. Continue along this path until broad gives way to farmland and you can see Hardley Hall off to your left. The path will then meet a wide farm track.

**WHILE YOU'RE THERE** ⓘ
**Hales Hall** was built by Sir James Hobart (Hobart in Australia was named after his family) in the 1470s. He was Attorney General to Henry VII and wealthy enough to raise himself a substantial mansion. It houses Reads Nursery and the national collection of citrus fruits. **Pettitt's Animal Adventure Park** is to the north east, and nearby **Raveningham Gardens** are well signposted from the village centre.

④ Turn left on the farm track. Go up a hill, passing **Hill Cottage** on your right-hand side. After about a mile (1.6km) the farm track ends at a lane. Turn left towards some woodland. Walk along this lane until you reach a line of ancient oak trees and a sign to your left stating 'Loddon 1¼'. Don't be tempted to take the left-hand footpath here, which heads to Chedgrave Common, since it doesn't end up where you want to be. Ignore the first turning on the left, signed 'No Through Road', and continue walking to the second.

⑤ Take this turning, signposted to the church. When you reach the church, look for the grassy footpath to the right which takes you back to Point ②, passed earlier in the walk. Retrace your steps along the footpath, go left on the main road, across the river and up the hill to the car park.

**WHAT TO LOOK FOR** ⓘ
A corner of the graveyard of **Holy Trinity Church** is unusual in that it has been set aside as a nature reserve. The church itself dates from the end of the 15th century and is very light and airy. Don't miss the painting of Sir James Hobart and his wife. There is only one all-timber **mill** in England, and that is at Loddon on the River Chet.

# Meres, Mosses and Moraines at Ellesmere

*A wonderful watery walk through Shropshire's lake district.*

| | |
|---|---|
| **•DISTANCE•** | 7¼ miles (11.7km) |
| **•MINIMUM TIME•** | 3hrs |
| **•ASCENT / GRADIENT•** | 180ft (55m) ▲ ▲ ▲ |
| **•LEVEL OF DIFFICULTY•** | 🏃 🏃 🏃 |
| **•PATHS•** | Field paths and canal tow path, 8 stiles |
| **•LANDSCAPE•** | Pastoral hills with glacial hollows containing small lakes |
| **•SUGGESTED MAP•** | aqua3 OS Explorer 241 Shrewsbury |
| **•START / FINISH•** | Grid reference: SJ 407344 |
| **•DOG FRIENDLINESS•** | Can run free on tow path, but under tight control elsewhere |
| **•PARKING•** | Castlefields car park opposite The Mere |
| **•PUBLIC TOILETS•** | Next to The Mere, almost opposite car park |

## BACKGROUND TO THE WALK

Ellesmere is one of those delightful little towns in which Shropshire specialises. It's well worth devoting some time to exploring it. But Ellesmere's biggest asset must be The Mere, the largest of all the meres that grace north Shropshire and south Cheshire. It attracts good numbers of water birds and is especially important for winter migrants such as wigeon, pochard, goosander and teal. It also has a large heronry occupied by breeding birds in spring and early summer.

On this walk you will explore about half of The Mere's shoreline and follow the tow path of the Llangollen Canal past Cole Mere and Blake Mere. Cole Mere is included within a country park and there is access from the tow path at Yell Bridge. If you want to explore Cole Mere, you can walk all the way round it. Blake Mere is particularly lovely; it's separated from the tow path only by a narrow strip of woodland, but there is no other access to it.

### Glacial Formations

The word mere is an Anglo-Saxon term for a lake. Unlike a normal lake, however, these meres have no stream flowing in or out of them. So how were they formed? It's a complex story but the Meres Visitor Centre has lots of information. What follows here is a simplified version. During the last ice age, the landscape was scoured by glaciers and when they retreated between 10,000 to 12,000 years ago, they left clay-lined hollows which retained melting ice, forming some of the meres. Others filled up later because they lay below the level of the water table. Water levels are maintained by natural drainage (groundwater percolation) from the surrounding countryside.

The landscape is composed of gentle hills that, combined with the meres, form a very pleasing scene. Technically, it consists of glacial drift, a mixture of clays, sands and gravels originally scoured from rocks by the glaciers as they moved south and east across Britain and then deposited in banks and mounds known as moraines as the glaciers retreated. In places, you can identify the origins of the glacial drift. Blue-black pebbles are slates from Snowdonia or Cumbria, and pale, speckled stones are granites from Cumbria or Scotland, while pink pebbles are from the local sandstone. These glacial meres are unique in this country and rare in global terms.

North Shropshire is also renowned for its mosses, which were created by the glaciers too, but they are filled with peat rather than water. You may well be familiar with the wonderful moss at Whixall, but there are several small mosses around Ellesmere too, though none with public access. The meres and mosses together form a wetland complex which, ecologically, is of national, if not international, significance.

# Walk 32 Directions

① Cross to **The Mere** and turn left. Pass **The Boathouse** and **Meres** **Visitor Centre** and walk towards town, until you come to **Cremorne Gardens**. Join a path that runs through trees close by the water's edge for about ¾ mile (1.2km).

**Walk 32**

② Leave the trees for a field and turn left, signposted 'Welshampton'. The path soon joins a track, which leads to **Crimps Farm**. Turn right past the farm buildings to cross a stile on the right of the track. Continue along another track.

③ The track leads into sheep pasture where you go straight on, guided by waymarkers and stiles. When you come to a field with a **trig pillar** in it, the waymarker is slightly misleading – ignore it and go straight across. In the next field you should aim for three prominent trees close together at the far side. As you approach them, turn left into the field corner.

**WHERE TO EAT AND DRINK** ⓘ

There is plenty of choice in Ellesmere. Special mention goes to **Vermeulen's** bakery/deli where you can buy the ingredients for a picnic. Or there's **The Boathouse** by The Mere, an unusual oak-beamed 1930s restaurant/tea room. There's a good range of snacks and drinks on offer, and dogs are welcome in the garden, which borders The Mere.

④ Go through a gate and descend by the right-hand hedge. When it turns a corner, go with it, to the right. Skirt a pool and keep going in the same direction on a grassy track, passing another pool. The track soon becomes much better defined and leads to a farm where you join a road.

⑤ Turn left and go straight on at a junction into **Welshampton**. Turn right on **Lyneal Lane** and follow it to a bridge over the **Llangollen Canal**. Descend steps to the tow path and turn right, passing under the bridge. Pass Lyneal Wharf, Cole Mere, Yell Wood and Blake Mere, then through **Ellesmere Tunnel**.

Beyond this are three footpaths signposted to The Mere. Take any of these short cuts if you wish, but to see a bit more of the canal, including the visitor moorings and marina, stay on the tow path.

**WHAT TO LOOK FOR** ⓘ

Many bird species can be seen, but one of the most endearing is the **great crested grebe**. This distinctive diving bird is nearly always present on the larger meres. You can recognise it by the crest on top of its head. In spring it has cute, stripy chicks which it sometimes carries on its back to give them a rest from all that paddling.

⑥ Arriving at **bridge 58**, further choices present themselves. You could extend this walk to include the signposted Wharf Circular Walk (recommended) or to explore the town (also recommended): just follow the signs. To return directly to The Mere, however, go up to the road and turn left.

⑦ Fork right on a road by **Blackwater Cottage**. Turn right at the top, then soon left at **Rose Bank**, up steps. Walk across the earthworks of the long-gone **Ellesmere Castle** and follow signs for The Mere or the car park.

**WHILE YOU'RE THERE** ⓘ

While The Mere is the highlight of **Ellesmere**, it would be a shame not to explore the town, especially the refurbished canal wharves and basin. There's lots to see, including the offices from which Thomas Telford directed the construction of the canal. Ellesmere was the headquarters of the Llangollen Canal (originally called the Ellesmere Canal) and so there are former workshops, warehouses and dry docks, while British Waterways still has an office and maintenance depot here.

# The Bard Taliesin and the Twin Lakes

*Here you can discover two very different lakes, one to inspire poets present and one that inspired bards of the past.*

| | |
|---|---|
| •DISTANCE• | 5 miles (8km) |
| •MINIMUM TIME• | 3hrs |
| •ASCENT / GRADIENT• | 656ft (200m) ▲▲▲ |
| •LEVEL OF DIFFICULTY• | 🚶 🚶 🚶 |
| •PATHS• | Clear paths and forestry tracks, 7 stiles |
| •LANDSCAPE• | Lake, afforested hillsides and woods |
| •SUGGESTED MAP• | aqua3 OS Explorer OL17 Snowdon |
| •START / FINISH• | Grid reference: SH 756618 |
| •DOG FRIENDLINESS• | Dogs could run free in forest areas |
| •PARKING• | Forestry car park, north of Llyn Crafnant |
| •PUBLIC TOILETS• | At car park |

## BACKGROUND TO THE WALK

Llyn Crafnant is serenely beautiful, and it's only 5 minutes from the car to its northern tip. Here, at the head of the 'valley of garlic', is a lake surrounded by woodland, lush pasture and craggy hills. The walk is easy too, on an undulating forestry track that gives a slightly elevated view of the lake. Little whitewashed cottages are arranged neatly in the lower pastures, while the hill slopes at the head of the valley are tinged with the russet of heather and the golden grey of the much-faulted crags which rise to the knobbly ridge crest. Here the summit of Crimpiau rules supreme.

### The Dead Lake

After rounding the lake the route climbs out of the valley, through the trees and zig-zags down into the upland hollow of Llyn Geirionydd. This is a wilder place altogether, one with barren hillsides and conifer plantations – sometimes there are waterskiers on the lake to contradict the wildness. Another lakeside path follows, sometimes almost dipping into the lapping waters. Round a corner you come to the spoil heaps of a huge old lead mine, one of many in the area. The lake has a secret – it has been poisoned and left sterile by these lead mines – you'll see no fish here!

### Taliesin and the Kings

On a grassy mound at the end of the lake stands an obelisk. Erected in 1850 it commemorates Taliesin, a 6th-century bard who has been linked to legends as colourful as his poems. Most scholars believe him to be of Irish descent and it is known he lived here at the northern end of Geirionydd. In those times bards would have been resident in the courts of many warlord kings, and Taliesin was said to have attended King Maelgwyn Gwynedd, one of the most sinful rulers in history, according to one of the local monks. After a fiery row the departing bard predicted that a yellow creature would rise from Morfa Rhianedd (Llandudno) and kill the King. It is known that when the King died in AD 547 there was an outbreak of yellow fever. Many of Taliesin's more fanciful poems recall tales of magic and mystery, and many of them relate to the heroics of the great King Arthur, who some believe was his one-time master. It is quite possible that he spent time in the court of Urien of Rheged, a northern leader whose kingdom occupied much of modern Cumbria and south west Scotland. Many people link Urien's deeds with those of the mythical Arthur.

The bardic traditions didn't die with Taliesin, for the Welsh poet, Gwilim Cowlyd organised an Eisteddfod in 1863, after a disagreement with the rules of the national event. It was held here until 1912, eight years after Cowlyd's death, and each year attracted many distinguished entries.

# Walk 33 **Directions**

① Turn right out of the car park and follow the lane to the north end of **Llyn Crafnant**. Turn right here, and follow the forestry track along the north west shores of the lake, before taking the lower left fork.

② Ignore the first stile on the left, and instead climb with the forestry track. Keep watch for a waymarked footpath on which you should descend left to pass beneath the cottage of **Hendre**. Go over a footbridge on the right, then turn left down a track past a couple of modern chalets.

**Walk 33**

③ Turn left along the road which heads back towards the lake. Leave this at a telephone box for a path, signposted 'Llyn Geirionydd' and waymarked with blue-capped posts. This climbs through the conifer forests and over the shoulder of **Mynydd Deulyn**.

④ Descend on a winding forestry track, still following the obvious blue-capped posts. Ignore the track forking to the right – that leads to Llyn Bychan.

⑤ On reaching the valley floor, leave the track to go over a step stile on the left. The path crosses a field beneath **Ty-newydd** cottage before tracing Llyn Geirionydd's shoreline.

At the northern end of the lake the path keeps to the right of a wall and meets a farm track.

⑥ Turn left along this, then right to the **Taliesin Monument**. Descend to a green path heading north west, then north, descending towards the Crafnant Valley.

⑦ Veer left to cross a ladder stile and follow an undulating path over rock and heather knolls.

⑧ The path eventually swings left to reach an old mine. Here, take the lower track on the right which descends back to the valley road and the forest car park.

# The Wildlife of Daneshill Lakes

*A very easy stroll around a watery nature reserve, reclaimed from old gravel pits near Retford in north Nottinghamshire.*

| | |
|---|---|
| **•DISTANCE•** | 3 miles (4.8km) |
| **•MINIMUM TIME•** | 1hr 30min |
| **•ASCENT / GRADIENT•** | Negligible ▲▲▲ |
| **•LEVEL OF DIFFICULTY•** | 🚶 🚶 🚶 |
| **•PATHS•** | Firm gravel tracks and woodland paths |
| **•LANDSCAPE•** | Small lakes and pools dotted around mixed woodland |
| **•SUGGESTED MAP•** | aqua3 OS Explorer 279 Doncaster |
| **•START / FINISH•** | Grid reference: SK 668865 |
| **•DOG FRIENDLINESS•** | On lead, except in designated 'dog run' area |
| **•PARKING•** | Nature reserve car park, Daneshill Road, signed from A638 |
| **•PUBLIC TOILETS•** | None on route (nearest in Retford) |

## BACKGROUND TO THE WALK

Daneshill Lakes Local Nature Reserve was created in the mid-1980s from a collection of shallow gravel extraction pits as part of a major reclamation project by Nottinghamshire County Council. It falls into two distinct parts, separated by Daneshill Road. To the south, leading off from the car park, is the more open and popular section, with benches and picnic tables, where windsurfers ply the main lake and anglers sit patiently by the shore. Coots and moorhens busy themselves among the reeds, and Canada geese, grebes and swans are a common sight. Across the road to the north is a more wooded and secluded area that is specially managed for wildlife. Here, on my first visit, I saw goldcrests and coal tits, and later on in the walk a commotion in the trees ahead was followed by a sparrowhawk shooting out at great speed. This is certainly the place to have your binoculars and identification book handy.

Despite being close to the road and a mainline railway, Daneshill Lakes provide a wonderful oasis for birdlife, partly because of the variety of different habitats – from open water and wetland through to scrub and woodland – so that you are almost as likely to see waders such as redshank and ringed plover as you are wood warblers, blackcaps and any of the three native British woodpeckers. But there is much else besides the birds, since dragonflies and damselflies take to the air when the summer temperatures rise sufficiently, and newts and toads revel in the wet and sheltered thickets.

### Star Millennium Pathway

This innovative route, which encompasses Daneshill Lakes, was designed as part of the local millennium celebrations and links the nearby villages of Scrooby, Ranskill and Torworth. All three are connected by the Great North Road (which used to be part of the A1, but is now reduced in status to the A638) as well as the railway, and historically have shared schools, churches and so on. The 'Star' is the name of the local newsletter produced and distributed among the villages.

**Walk 34**

### The Pilgrim Fathers Heritage

Today the small village of Scrooby (3 miles/4.8km north of Daneshill Lakes) seems a very quiet and unassuming sort of place, but its significance in history is confirmed by the name of the pub – the Pilgrim Fathers.

Local man William Brewster, who lived at the manor house, rebelled against the orthodox Church by actively promoting what was called Separatism. But early 17th-century England wasn't exactly tolerant of religious dissenters, and Brewster ended up fleeing to Holland. In the autumn of 1620 he set sail for North America on board the *Mayflower*, with the other so-called Pilgrim Fathers, to start a new life. The rest, as they say, is history.

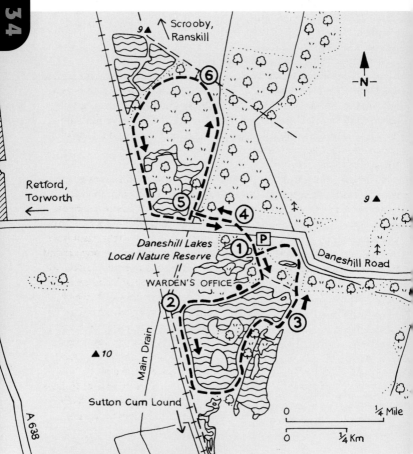

## Walk 34 **Directions**

① From the car park go through the main gate and ahead past the notice board on the wide gravel track. At the junction swing right, so that the large lake opens up on your left. Go past the **warden's office** and sailing club hut along the water's edge.

② Approaching the railway look for the two large track-side signs which read 'Edinburgh 350 miles'. (Fortunately today's walk is a little less ambitious.) The first left turn is a continuation of the lakeside path, and the second left is via the dog-run next to the railway. Both join up 350yds (320m) later and resume the easy tour around the main lake, past large bushes of rose hip. A second, smaller lake opens up on the right.

③ When you meet the fence at the end, with an open field beyond, turn left. As this bears left after 300yds (274m) take the small grassy path into the woods half right, as indicated by a small wooden post bearing the letters 'MM'. This is a wildlife trail created for the millennium and designed in particular for use by local school groups. It wanders happily through the bushes and trees and beside a small stream (look out for the pond-dipping platform), and when it finally emerges from the undergrowth turn right and right again to return to the car park. Continue via the small path through the trees to the left of the road entrance and cross the road.

④ Go through the gateway on the opposite side and turn left on to a wide track, indicated 'Easy Access to Reserve' (ignore the footpath to the right). Follow this track until you reach a wooden footbridge. Go across, then turn right and walk along to reach the notice board by the woodland pond.

⑤ Continue to follow this easy and obvious track through the reserve, keeping the ditch and stream on your right-hand side and ignoring an inviting turning to the right across a footbridge.

⑥ Unless you want to make a diversion at this point to visit Ranskill as well, ignore the right turn for the Millennium Pathway, and instead stick to the main path as it completes a giant loop around the entire nature reserve. Look out for the shallow pools and scrapes among the undergrowth, which, unless they've dried out in hot weather, are a focus for creatures such as frogs and beetles. After about a mile (1.6km) or so you arrive back at the wooden footbridge. Turn right here to cross it, go through the gateway to the road and cross over to return to the car park.

**Walk 35**

# Round Combs Reservoir and Across Dickie's Meadow

*A quiet corner of north west Derbyshire, hidden between the Goyt and Chapel-en-le-Frith.*

| | |
|---|---|
| •DISTANCE• | 3 miles (4.8km) |
| •MINIMUM TIME• | 2hrs 30min |
| •ASCENT / GRADIENT• | 164ft (50m) ▲▲▲ |
| •LEVEL OF DIFFICULTY• | 🚶🚶 🚶 🚶 |
| •PATHS• | Can be muddy, quite a few stiles |
| •LANDSCAPE• | Lakes, meadows, and high moors |
| •SUGGESTED MAP• | aqua3 OS Outdoor Leisure 24 White Peak |
| •START / FINISH• | Grid reference: SK 033797 |
| •DOG FRIENDLINESS• | Farmland – dogs should be kept on leads |
| •PARKING• | Combs reservoir car park |
| •PUBLIC TOILETS• | None on route |

## BACKGROUND TO THE WALK

Combs lies in a quite corner of north west Derbyshire, off the road between Chapel-en-le-Frith and Whaley Bridge and beneath the sombre crag-fringed slopes of Combs Moss. I wouldn't have known about the place if my wife Nicola hadn't been invited to sail in the Byte Open held at the local reservoir. I thought I'd have a brief wander while she prepared for the first race, but my wanderings lasted well into the afternoon. I'd discovered a fine little corner of Derbyshire, tucked well away from the crowds of Castleton, or the hordes of Hathersage.

### Combs Reservoir

The route starts by the west side of the dam on a narrow path between the lake and Meveril Brook. Red campion, and thickets of dog rose line the path, which rounds the reservoir to its southern tip. Here I saw a pair of great crested grebes swimming among the rushes. Beyond the reservoir the path tucks under the railway, which brings to mind a mysterious story concerning Ned Dixon, who lived in nearby Tunstead Farm. Ned, or Dickie as he was known, was brutally murdered by his cousin. Locals say his spirit lived on in his skull, which was left outside to guard against intruders. Strange things were said to happen when anybody tried to remove the skull. It is also claimed that the present road from Combs to Chapel was constructed because the railway bridge would not stand over Dane Hey Road. After the first bridge was completed it collapsed, burying the workmen's tools. This was blamed on the skull: Dickie had been against the railway going across Tunstead land.

### Combs

A lane with hedges of honeysuckle and hawthorn winds into the village of Combs, where a handful of stone-built cottages are centred on the welcoming Beehive Inn. Combs' most famous son is Herbert Froode. He made his name in automotive engineering as one of the inventors of the brake lining. Starting out in the early 1890s he developed woven cotton brakes for horse drawn wagons, but his ideas didn't really take off until 1897 when the first motor buses emerged. Froode applied his knowledge of brakes to this much greater challenge and by the end of the century had won a contract to supply brake linings for the new London omnibuses. Ferodo, his company, is an anagram of his surname.

Through the village the route takes to the hillsides. Now Combs Reservoir, which is spread beneath your feet, looks every bit a natural lake. Beyond it are the plains of Manchester and the hazy blue West Pennine horizon. In the other direction the gritstone cliffs of Combs Edge, which look rather like those of Kinder Scout, overshadow the sullen combe of Pyegreave Brook. This very pleasing walk ends as it starts, by the shores of the reservoir. If you look along the line of the dam towards the right of two farms, you'll see where Dickie lived. He's probably watching you, too.

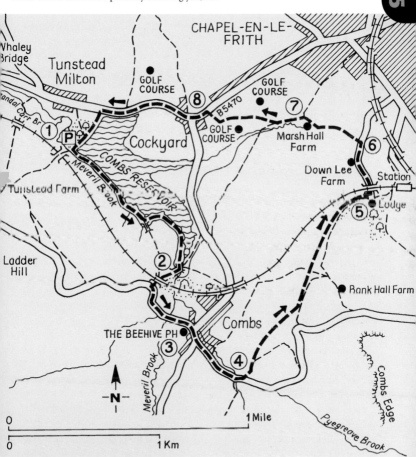

# Walk 35 Directions

① Follow the path from the dam along the reservoir's western shore, ignoring the first footbridge over **Meveril Brook**.

② As the reservoir narrows the path traverses small fields, then comes to another footbridge over the brook. This time cross it and head south across another field. Beyond a foot tunnel under the Buxton line railway, the path

**Walk 35**

reaches a narrow hedge-lined country lane. Turn left along the lane into **Combs** village.

③ Past the Beehive Inn in the village centre, take the lane straight ahead, then the left fork, signposted to **Dove Holes**. This climbs out of the village towards Combs Edge.

---

**WHILE YOU'RE THERE** ⓘ

Take a good look around **Chapel-en-le-Frith**, a fine market town with a cobbled market square and the 14th-century Church of St Thomas à Becket. In 1648 1,500 Scottish soldiers were taken prisoner and locked in the church after the Battle of Ribbleton Moor. Forty-eight of them died in what was to be known as the Black Hole of Derbyshire.

---

④ Take the second footpath on the left, which begins at a muddy clearing just beyond **Millway Cottage**. Go through the stile and climb on a partially slabbed path through a narrow grassy enclosure. After 200yds (183m) the path emerges on a pastured spur overlooking the huge comb of **Pygreave Brook**. Climb the pathless spur and go through gateways in the next two boundary walls before following a wall on the right. Ignore a gate in this wall – that's a path to **Bankhall Farm**, but stay with the narrow path raking across rough grassy hillslopes with the railway line and the reservoir below left.

⑤ The path comes down to a rutted vehicle track running alongside the railway. This joins a narrow lane just short of the **Lodge** (grid ref 053794). Turn left to go under the railway and north to **Down Lea Farm**.

⑥ Turn left through a kissing gate 200yds (183m) beyond the farmhouse. The signposted path follows an overgrown hedge towards **Marsh Hall Farm**. The fields are very boggy on the final approaches. On reaching the farm complex turn right over a stile and follow a track heading north west.

⑦ After 200yds (183m) turn left on a field path that heads west to a stile at the edge of the **Chapel-en-le-Frith golf course**. Waymarking arrows show the way across the fairway. The stile marking the exit from the golf course is 300yds (274m) short of the clubhouse. You then cross a small field to the B5470.

⑧ Turn left along the road (there's a pavement on the far side), and follow it past the **Hanging Gate pub** at **Cockyard**. After passing the entrance to the sailing club, turn left across the reservoir's dam and back to the car park.

---

**WHERE TO EAT AND DRINK** ⓘ

The **Beehive** at Combs is a splendid little pub serving fine bar meals. Alternatively, there's the more formal **Hanging Gate Inn** at Cockyard just before you get back to the reservoir dam.

---

**WHAT TO LOOK FOR** ⓘ

On a bright winter's day in 1995 a group of birdwatchers saw something they hadn't been expecting. While wandering by the hedge along the west shores of the reservoir they came across some huge clawed footprints 3½ins (89mm) wide, which were sunk deep into the mud. These didn't belong to any dog. After studying the photographs they had taken it became obvious that a huge cat had been on the prowl – probably the infamous Peak Panther that has had many sightings on the nearby hills above Chinley and Hayfield.

# A Peak Experience Around Dove Stones

*A magnificent walk along the edge of the moors is the centrepiece of this grand outing.*

| | |
|---|---|
| •DISTANCE• | 8 miles (12.9km) |
| •MINIMUM TIME• | 3hrs |
| •ASCENT / GRADIENT• | 1,296ft (395m) ▲▲▲ |
| •LEVEL OF DIFFICULTY• | 🚶 🚶 🚶 |
| •PATHS• | Mostly on good tracks but with some rocky sections, occasionally very steep, 2 stiles |
| •LANDSCAPE• | Open and exposed moors, with sheltered valleys |
| •SUGGESTED MAP• | aqua3 OS Explorer OL1 Dark Peak |
| •START / FINISH• | Grid reference: SE 013034 |
| •DOG FRIENDLINESS• | Condition of access to moors is dogs must be on leads |
| •PARKING• | Dovestone Reservoir, pay at weekends |
| •PUBLIC TOILETS• | At car park |

## BACKGROUND TO THE WALK

Cheshire's stake in the Peak District National Park is modest, but on this walk you can sample the vast moors so characteristic of the Dark Peak. These are notorious for tough walking over peat and heather, but this is an easy promenade along the edge of the moors; the only hard part is the steep ascent of Birchen Clough.

### Skirting the Reservoirs

It starts easily, alongside a series of reservoirs, allowing you to look up to the crags that necklace the skyline. Dove Stones, directly above the start, has a natural edge as well as a large, long-abandoned quarry. You might also ponder what the King of Tonga was doing at Yeoman Hey Dam in 1981. Above the last of the reservoirs, you follow the Greenfield Brook, climbing gently. The forked tower dubbed the Trinnacle is eye-catching – and you'll get a closer look soon. Don't miss the water-sculpted rocks in the bed of the stream.

### The Dark Peak Moors

Now you make the transition from valley to moor, by the steep ascent of Birchen Clough. The steepest step is alongside a small waterfall and, if it really looks uninviting, backtrack a short way to pick up a path (still steep) which traverses above the obstacle. The easier upper reaches of the Clough, and the flanking slopes leading out on to the moor, are home to substantial numbers of Canada geese.

You reach the edge of the moor close to Raven Stones and soon find yourself looking down on the unmistakable Trinnacle. It's a great foreground for photographs and looks even better with someone standing on the top, but the ascent can only be recommended to experienced scramblers. You have to sidle along an exposed ledge below the lowest top; then it's easier climbing to the middle one but there's a long stride across a deep gap to the highest – and it seems a lot longer coming back!

### Above Dove Stones

The edge is less defined for a time and you cross a vague shoulder past Ashway Cross before clarity is restored. Above Dove Stones the main path keeps back from the edge, but this is magnificently exposed if you don't mind that sort of thing. Just beyond is the isolated tor of Fox Stone. Here a plaque commemorates two Dark Peak climbers who were killed in the Italian Dolomites.

### Rough Shelter

In wild weather, the ruins of Bramley's Cot, once a shooters' hut, provide the best shelter if you need somewhere to take on food and drink. The end wall still stands and you can see the carved sockets where the roof timbers were set. There's still a mile (1.6km) of moor-edge to go before you drop into the valley of the Chew Brook that gives easy walking back to where you began.

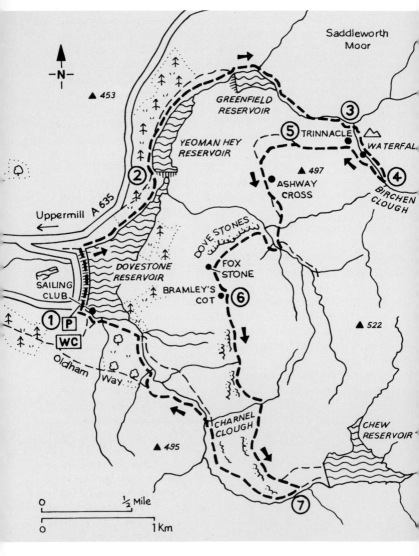

Walk 36

# Walk 36 Directions

① Cross the dam and continue just above the shoreline. Climb up near the end then drop down again to **Yeoman Hey Dam**.

② Follow the left side of the reservoir. At a fork keep to the higher path, rising gently to the next dam. Follow the left side of **Greenfield Reservoir** and then wind on up the narrowing valley. Climb more steeply to more waterworks where the valley forks.

---

**WHERE TO EAT AND DRINK** ⓘ

There's usually a tea/hot dog van at the car park in summer and at weekends. The Church Inn, Uppermill (head down the A635, then keep turning right) is a lively place that brews its own beer.

---

③ Skirt rightwards above a tunnel entrance, then take a rough path up the right branch, **Birchen Clough**. Cross the stream when a steep little crag blocks the way. The path is steep and rough, with one awkward step just below a 20ft (6m) cascade. Above this the clough is shallower and less steep. After some wet patches the clough opens out, with nearly-level ground on the right.

④ Cross the stream and go up right to a marshy terrace. Keep climbing to the right where the slope is less steep. A path materialises just below

---

**WHAT TO LOOK FOR** ⓘ

The Peak District is at the centre of British rock climbing. The crags of Ravenstones and Dove Stones are not the most popular in the area, but in good weather you're quite likely to see a few climbers here. The boulders alongside the plantation near the end of the walk are also used for intense micro-climbs.

---

the plateau edge, rising gently towards the crags. Cross a stile then follow the top of the crags past the **Trinnacle**. After about 440yds (402m) the path forks.

⑤ Go left to a stile, with a cairn just beyond, and a near-level path across the moor. Above a ruin, bear left up a short stony slope, reaching the plateau near **Ashway Cross**. Continue along the edge of the moor; the path keeps generally level, swinging left to cross a stream then back right. Where the path is unclear follow the boundary between peat and rock. The main path keeps a discreet distance from the edge of **Dove Stones**. Beyond the isolated **Fox Stone** the route bears a little left, passing the remains of a stone hut below a crag, **Bramley's Cot**.

---

**WHILE YOU'RE THERE** ⓘ

Uppermill is the 'capital' of the Saddleworth district, a cluster of no fewer than 14 villages, many of whose inhabitants still feel their first loyalty is to Yorkshire. The Saddleworth Museum is housed in a former mill alongside the canal at Uppermill.

---

⑥ Continue along the moor edge, crossing **Charnel Clough**. The path still keeps generally level, swinging left above the Chew valley until the dam of the Chew Reservoir appears ahead. Watch out for the unfenced edge of a small quarry. Skirt round this and down the grass slope beyond to the reservoir road.

⑦ Descend the road until the gradient eases. Just before a gate, drop down left to a ridge. Take the obvious rising path beyond. Slant down right before a plantation, past some boulders. Rejoin the road past the **sailing club** to the car park.

# Rocks and Water at Anglezarke

*A landscape shaped by quarries and reservoirs, full of interest both historical and natural.*

| | |
|---|---|
| •DISTANCE• | 7 miles (11.3km) |
| •MINIMUM TIME• | 2hrs 30min |
| •ASCENT / GRADIENT• | 689ft (210m) |
| •LEVEL OF DIFFICULTY• | |
| •PATHS• | Mostly good tracks with some field paths, 20 stiles |
| •LANDSCAPE• | Woodland, reservoirs, open valleys and farmland |
| •SUGGESTED MAP• | aqua3 OS Explorer 287 West Pennine Moors |
| •START / FINISH• | Grid reference: SD 621161 |
| •DOG FRIENDLINESS• | Can run free on reservoir tracks, sheep elsewhere |
| •PARKING• | Large car park at Anglezarke |
| •PUBLIC TOILETS• | Nearest at Rivington |

## BACKGROUND TO THE WALK

A string of reservoirs moats the western side of the high moors of Anglezarke and Rivington and quarries scar their flanks. This is not a pristine landscape by any stretch of the imagination, yet today it is seen by many as an oasis of tranquillity close to busy towns and a motorway.

### Reclaimed by Nature

A gentle start just above the shores of Anglezarke Reservoir leads to Lester Mill Quarry, which was worked until the 1930s. The quarry wall is imposing, but somewhat vegetated, and the rock is loose in places. It is much less popular with climbers than Anglezarke Quarry. The name is one reminder that this valley was once a thriving agricultural community. The mill, which served the whole valley, was drowned by the reservoir in 1855. Cheap imports further weakened the rural economy. Today there is only one working farm east of the reservoir.

The route continues through a mix of woodland and pasture to the head of the lake, then heads up the valley below steep, bouldery Stronstrey Bank. There's another quarry high on the right near the end of the bank, seemingly guarded by a number of gaunt, dead trees. Just beyond is another, set further back. Just beyond this an impressive spillway testifies to the potential power of Dean Black Brook.

### A Busy Industrial Village

Now you cross The Goit, a canal that feeds the reservoir, to White Coppice cricket ground. There's a small reservoir just above and you pass others on the way down to the present-day hamlet. These served the mills that flourished here for well over a century. Along with the quarries at Stronstrey Bank these made White Coppice a busy industrial village with a population which may have approached 200. The mill closed in 1914 and little remains today. The railway closed in the late 1950s, the school in 1963 and the church in 1984. This sounds like a story of decline yet today many people would see White Coppice as an idyllic place to live, a fact reflected in the local house prices.

### View to Winter Hill

After White Coppice you climb to Healey Nab. Trees obscure what must have been a fine all-round view from the highest point, but there's a good southward prospect from the large cairn on Grey Heights. Winter Hill is the highest of the moors, unmistakable with its TV towers. The main mast is just over 1,000ft (305m) tall, so you could argue that its tip is the highest point in Lancashire. The string of reservoirs is also well displayed and you get a bird's eye view of Chorley.

The walk finishes across the Anglezarke dam and then, to minimise road walking, makes a short climb to the small Yarrow Reservoir. The final descent gives an opportunity to look into Anglezarke Quarry.

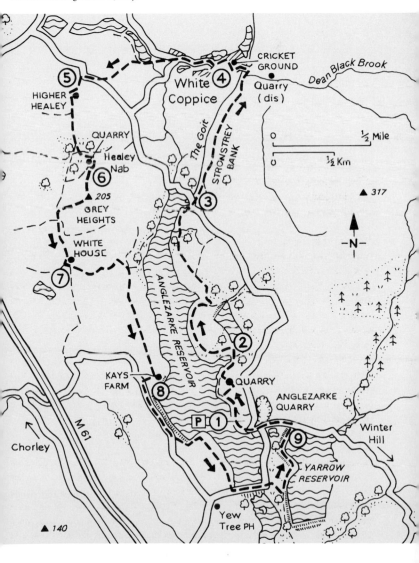

**Walk 37**

**Walk 37 Directions**

① Leave the car park by a kissing gate and follow a track near the water. Fork right, through **Lester Mill Quarry**, then go right, and straight on at the next junction. The track climbs a steep rise.

---

**WHERE TO EAT AND DRINK** ⓘ

The **Yew Tree**, at Lane Ends, 250yds (229m) from the Anglezarke dam, lacks cask beer but has a cosy atmosphere and a choice of bar food or a restaurant menu. Families are welcome and there's outside seating for those with dogs.

---

② Go through a gap on the left, on a bend. The path traverses a wooded slope. Descend steps, join a wider track and go left. Beyond a stile follow a narrower path until it meets a road.

③ Go left 50yds (46m) to a kissing gate. Follow a track up the valley below **Stronstrey Bank**. Cross a bridge then go through a kissing gate and over another bridge to **White Coppice cricket ground**.

④ Bear left up a lane, then follow tarmac into **White Coppice** hamlet. Cross a bridge by the post-box. Follow a stream then go up left by a reservoir. Bear left to a stile. Cross the next field to its top right corner and go right on a lane. Where it bends right go left up a track.

---

**WHAT TO LOOK FOR** ⓘ

Subtle differences in the nature of the **rock** can be seen in the different quarries. These were significant for the uses to which the stone could be put. Parts of Anglezarke Quarry are 'massive' – there are very few cracks. Some of the rock here is especially pure and was used to line blast furnaces.

---

⑤ Skirt **Higher Healey**, follow field edges, then angle up left into dark plantations. Fork left just inside, and ascend to an old quarry. Follow its rim for three-quarters of the way round then bear away left through a larch plantation.

⑥ Go left on a clear path then right to the large cairn on **Grey Heights**. Descend slightly right, winding down past a small plantation, and join a wider green track. Bear left over a small rise then follow a track to a lane by **White House farm**.

---

**WHILE YOU'RE THERE** ⓘ

On most days, but especially at weekends, there's a very good chance of seeing rock climbers in **Anglezarke Quarry**. It's one of the most popular venues in Lancashire. A recent guidebook listed 165 routes ranging in severity from Difficult (which isn't) to E6 (which is), and more have been added since.

---

⑦ Cross a stile on the left, below the farmyard wall, then bear left to the corner of the field. Cross the stile on the left then up the field edge and join a confined path. From a stile on the right follow trees along the field edge to a rough track. Go right and straight on to **Kays Farm**.

⑧ Go right down a track then left on a lane below the reservoir wall. As the lane angles away, go left over a stile then skirt the reservoir until pushed away from the water by a wood. Join the road across the dam. Go through a gap and up a steep track. Go left at the top round **Yarrow Reservoir** to a road.

⑨ Go left, passing the entrance to **Anglezarke Quarry**, to a junction. Go right, and the car park entrance is on the first bend.

# Along the Wharfe to a Victorian Spa Town

*From Addingham to Ilkley, along a stretch of the lovely River Wharfe.*

| | |
|---|---|
| •DISTANCE• | 5½ miles (8.8km) |
| •MINIMUM TIME• | 2hrs 30min |
| •ASCENT / GRADIENT• | 197ft (60m) ▲ ▲ ▲ |
| •LEVEL OF DIFFICULTY• | 🚶 🚶 🚶 |
| •PATHS• | Riverside path and field paths, some road walking, 7 stiles |
| •LANDSCAPE• | Rolling country and the River Wharfe |
| •SUGGESTED MAP• | aqua3 OS Explorer 297 Lower Wharfedale |
| •START / FINISH• | Grid reference: SE 084498 |
| •DOG FRIENDLINESS• | Keep on lead on minor roads |
| •PARKING• | Lay-by at eastern end of Addingham, on bend where North Street becomes Bark Lane by information panel |
| •PUBLIC TOILETS• | Ilkley |

## BACKGROUND TO THE WALK

Addingham is not one of those compact Yorkshire villages that huddles around a village green. The houses extend for a mile (1.6km) on either side of the main street, with St Peter's Church at the eastern end of the village, close to the river. So it's no surprise that the village used to known as 'Long Addingham', and that it is actually an amalgamation of three separate communities that grew as the textile trades expanded. Having been by-passed in recent years, Addingham is now a quiet backwater.

Within 50 years, from the end of the 17th century, Addingham's population quadrupled, from 500 to 2,000. Even here, at the gateway to the Yorkshire Dales, the textile industries flourished. At the height of the boom, there were six woollen mills in the village. Low Mill, built in 1787, was the scene of a riot by a band of Luddites – weavers and shearers who objected to their jobs being done by machines. Though the mill itself was demolished in 1972, more houses were added to the mill-hands' cottages to create Low Mill Village, a pleasant riverside community.

### Ilkley

Visitors from, say, Bath or Cheltenham should feel quite at home in Ilkley, a town that seems to have more in common with Harrogate, its even posher neighbour to the north, than with the textile towns of West Yorkshire. The Romans established an important fort here – believed to be 'Olicana' – on a site close to where the parish church is today. Two Roman altars were incorporated into the base of the church tower, and in the churchyard can be found three Anglo-Saxon crosses that date back to the 9th century. One of the few tangible remains of the Roman settlement is a short stretch of wall near the handsome Manor House, which is now a museum.

Like nearby Harrogate, Ilkley's fortunes changed dramatically with the discovery of medicinal springs. During the reign of Queen Victoria, the great and the good would come here to 'take the waters' and socialise at the town's hydros and hotels. Visitor numbers increased with the coming of the railway, and included such luminaries as Madame Tussaud, George Bernard Shaw and Charles Darwin, taking a well-earned rest after the publication of the *Origin of Species*.

With its open-air swimming pool and riverside promenades, Ilkley was almost an inland resort. Though we have replaced water cures with more sophisticated quackery, Ilkley remains a prosperous town, unashamedly dedicated to the good things of life.

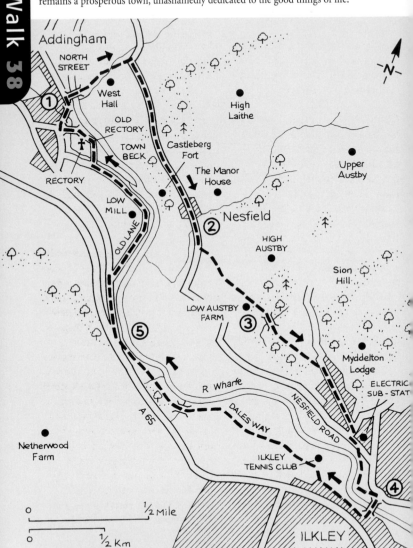

## Walk 38 **Directions**

① Walk 50yds (46m) up the road, and take stone steps down to the right, (signed '**Dales Way**'). Bear

immediately right again, and cross the **River Wharfe** on a suspension bridge. Follow a metalled path along a field edge. Cross a stream and join a metalled track between walls that soon emerges at a minor

> **WHERE TO EAT AND DRINK** ⓘ
> In Addingham try the **Sailor's Arms** or
> the **Fleece** for traditional pub food. At the
> bottom end of Ilkley you are close to the
> **'The Taps'** or the Ilkley Moor Vaults as it
> officially called, and the **Riverside Hotel**,
> which is particularly child-friendly.

road by a sharp bend. Go right
here; after about ½ mile (800m)
of road walking you reach the little
community of **Nesfield**.

② About 100yds (91m) beyond the
last house, and immediately after
the road crosses a stream, bear left
up a stony track (signed as a
footpath to **High Austby**).
Immediately take a stile between
two gates. Cross the field ahead,
keeping parallel to the road
(ignoring a track going left, uphill).
There is no obvious path; follow the
wall on your right, over a stile.
Beyond a small conifer plantation,
take a ladder stile in the fence ahead
to keep left of **Low Austby Farm**.

③ Cross a footbridge over a stream;
beyond a stile you enter woodland.
Follow a path downhill, leaving the
wood by another step stile. Follow
a fence uphill, then cross the middle
of a field to locate a stile at the far
end, to enter more woodland.
Follow an obvious path through the
trees, before reaching a road via a
wall stile. Go right, downhill, to
reach a road junction. Go right
again, crossing **Nesfield Road**, and
take a path to the left of an
electricity sub-station. You have a
few minutes of riverside walking
before you reach Ilkley's old stone
bridge.

④ Cross the bridge. This is your
opportunity to explore the spa town
of **Ilkley**. Otherwise you should
turn right, immediately after the

bridge, on to a riverside path (from
here back to **Addingham** you are
following the well-signed **Dales
Way**). You soon continue along a
lane, passing **Ilkley Tennis Club**.
Opposite the clubhouse, take a
footpath to the left, through a
kissing gate, and across pasture. You
have seven more kissing gates to
negotiate before you are back by the
**River Wharfe** again. Cross a stream
on a footbridge, and enter
woodland. Cross another stream to
meet a stony track. Go right,
downhill, on this track to the river.
Through another kissing gate, you
follow a grassy path (with
woodland and a fence to your left)
before joining the old A65 road.
Thanks to the by-pass it is now
almost empty of traffic.

⑤ Follow the road by the riverside.
After almost ½ mile (800m) of road
walking, go right, just before a row
of terraced houses, on to **Old Lane**.
Pass between the houses of a new
development – **Low Mill Village** –
to locate a riverside path, now
metalled, at the far side. Once you
have passed the Rectory on the left,
and the grounds of the **Old Rectory**
on your right, look for a kissing
gate on the right. Take steps and
follow the path to a tiny arched
bridge over **Town Beck**. You have
a grassy path across pasture, in
front of the church, before taking
another bridge, between houses,
to re-emerge on **North Street** in
**Addingham**.

> **WHILE YOU'RE THERE** ⓘ
> Addingham lies at the north western
> edge of the county. Just a mile to the
> north you enter the Yorkshire Dales
> National Park. By following the B6160
> you soon come to **Bolton Abbey**, with
> its priory ruins in an idyllic setting by a
> bend in the River Wharfe.

**Walk 39**

# Dalesfolk Traditions in Hubberholme

*From JB Priestley's favourite Dales village, along Langstrothdale and back via a limestone terrace.*

| | |
|---|---|
| •DISTANCE• | 5 miles (8km) |
| •MINIMUM TIME• | 2hrs |
| •ASCENT / GRADIENT• | 394ft (120m) ▲▲▲ |
| •LEVEL OF DIFFICULTY• | 🚶 🚶 🚶 |
| •PATHS• | Field paths and tracks, steep after Yockenthwaite, 11 stiles |
| •LANDSCAPE• | Streamside paths and limestone terrace |
| •SUGGESTED MAP• | aqua3 OS Outdoor Leisure 30 Yorkshire Dales – Northern & Central |
| •START / FINISH• | Grid reference: SD 927782 |
| •DOG FRIENDLINESS• | Dogs should be on lead, except on section between Yockenthwaite and Cray |
| •PARKING• | Beside river in village, opposite church (not church parking) |
| •PUBLIC TOILETS• | None on route |

## BACKGROUND TO THE WALK

Literary pilgrims visit Hubberholme to see the George Inn, where JB Priestley could often be found enjoying the local ale, and the churchyard, the last resting place for his ashes, as he requested. He chose an idyllic spot. Set at the foot of Langstrothdale, Hubberholme is a cluster of old farmhouses and cottages surrounding the church. Norman in origin, St Michael's was once flooded so badly that fish were seen swimming in the nave. One vicar of Hubberholme is said to have carelessly baptised a child Amorous instead of Ambrose, a mistake that, once entered in the parish register, couldn't be altered. Amorous Stanley used his memorable name later in life as part of his stock-in-trade as a hawker.

### Church Wood

Hubberholme church's best treasures are of wood. The rood loft above the screen is one of only two surviving in Yorkshire, (the other is at Flamborough, far away on the east coast). Once holding figures of Christ on the Cross, St Mary and St John, it dates from 1558, when such examples of Popery were fast going out of fashion. It still retains some of its once-garish colouring of red, gold and black. Master-carver Robert Thompson provided almost all the rest of the furniture in 1934 – look for his mouse trademark on each piece.

### Ancient Yockenthwaite and Remote Cray

Yockenthwaite's name, said to have been derived from an ancient Irish name, Eogan, conjures up images of the ancient past. Norse settlers were here more than 1,000 years ago – and even earlier settlers have left their mark, a Bronze Age stone circle a little further up the valley. The hamlet now consists of a few farm buildings beside the bridge over the Wharfe at the end of Langstrothdale Chase, a Norman hunting ground which used to have its own forest laws and punishments. You walk along a typical Dales limestone terrace to reach Cray, on the road over from Bishopdale joining Wharfedale to Wensleydale. Here is another huddle of farmhouses, around the White Lion Inn. You then follow the Cray Gill downstream, past a series of small cascades. For a more spectacular waterfall, head up the road from the inn a little way to Cray High Bridge.

### Burning the Candle

Back in Hubberholme, the George Inn was once the vicarage. It is the scene each New Year's Day of an ancient auction. It begins with the lighting of a candle, after which the auctioneer asks for bids for the year's tenancy of the 'Poor Pasture', a 16 acre (7.2ha) field behind the inn. All bids have to be completed before the candle burns out. In the days when the George housed the vicar, he ran the auction. Today a local auctioneer takes the role, and a merry time is had by all. The proceeds from the auction go to help the old people of the village.

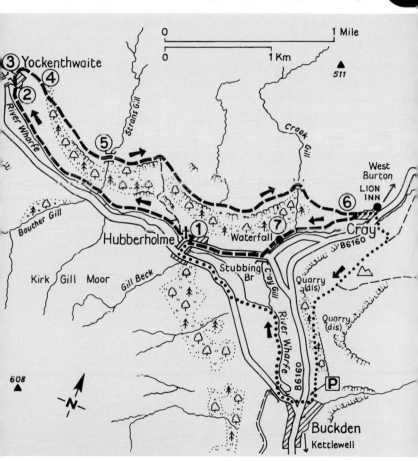

## Walk 39 Directions

① Go through a **Dales Way** signed gate near the east end of the church, bend left and then take the lower path, signed '**Yockenthwaite**'. Walk beside the river for 1¼ miles (2km) through three stiles, a gate and two more stiles. The path eventually rises to another stone stile into **Yockenthwaite**.

Walk 39

② Go through the stile and bend left to a wooden gate. Continue through a farm gate by a sign to **Deepdale and Beckermonds**. Before the track reaches a bridge go right and swing round to a sign to **Cray and Hubberholme**.

③ Go up the hill and, as the track curves right, continue to follow the **Cray and Hubberholme** sign. Part-way up the hill go right at a footpath sign through a wooden gate in a fence.

④ Go through a second gate to a footpath sign and ascend the hillside. Go through a gap in a wall by another signpost and follow the obvious path through several gaps in crossing walls. Go over two stone stiles and ascend again to a footbridge between stiles.

⑤ Cross the bridge and continue through woodland to another stile. Wind round the head of the valley and follow the signpost to **Cray**.

Go over a footbridge. The footpath winds its way down the valley side. Go through a gate and straight ahead across meadow land to a gateway on to a track, and on to a stone barn.

⑥ Bend to the right beyond the barn, down to a public footpath sign to **Stubbing Bridge**. Go down the path between stone walls and through a wooden gate and on to the grassy hillside. Pass another footpath sign and continue downhill to meet the stream by a waterfall.

⑦ Continue along the streamside path through woodland. Go over a wooden stile and on past a barn to a stone stile on to the road. Turn right along the road back to the parking place in **Hubberholme**.

**WHILE YOU'RE THERE** ℹ

If you've the energy, a walk to the summit of nearby **Buckden Pike** will reward you with fine views and a memorial to five Polish airmen whose plane crashed there in November 1942. One man survived the crash, following a fox's footprints through the snow down to safety at a farm. The cross he erected has a fox's head set in the base as thanksgiving. Buckden Pike is best climbed up the track called Walden Road from Starbotton.

**WHAT TO LOOK FOR** ℹ

A number of barns in the area have been converted to become holiday accommodation **bunk barns**. An initiative set up by the Yorkshire Dales National Park Authority and the Countryside Commission in 1979, the aim is to solve two problems – how to preserve the now-redundant barns that are so vital a part of the Dales landscape, and a lack of simple accommodation for walkers. Also known as stone tents, these bunkhouse barns offer farmers an alternative to letting the barns decay. They add basic amenities for cooking, washing and sleeping (and sometimes extras like comfortable chairs!) and let them to families or groups at a realistic nightly rate. They help to keep the farms viable, and both walkers and farmers benefit in other ways, too; meeting each other helps each to appreciate the needs and hopes of the other. As one farmer's wife said, 'We've made a lot of friends though the barn'.

# Semerwater – A Legendary Glacial Lake

*Legends – perhaps with a basis in dim and distant truth – surround Yorkshire's biggest natural lake.*

| | |
|---|---|
| **•DISTANCE•** | 5 miles (8km) |
| **•MINIMUM TIME•** | 2hrs |
| **•ASCENT / GRADIENT•** | 853ft (260m) ▲ ▲ ▲ |
| **•LEVEL OF DIFFICULTY•** | 🚶🚶 🚶🚶 🚶 |
| **•PATHS•** | Field paths and tracks, steep ascent from Marsett, 19 stiles |
| **•LANDSCAPE•** | Valley, lake and fine views over Wensleydale |
| **•SUGGESTED MAP•** | aqua3 OS Outdoor Leisure 30 Yorkshire Dales – Northern & Central |
| **•START / FINISH•** | Grid reference: SD 921875 |
| **•DOG FRIENDLINESS•** | Dogs should be on leads |
| **•PARKING•** | Car park at the north end of the lake |
| **•PUBLIC TOILETS•** | None on route |

## BACKGROUND TO THE WALK

Semerwater was formed as the result of the end of the last Ice Age. Glacial meltwater attempted to drain away down the valley the glacier had gouged out of the limestone, but was prevented from doing so by a wall of boulder clay, dumped by the glacier itself, across the valley's end. So the water built up, forming a lake which once stretched 3 miles (4.8km) up Raydale. Natural silting has gradually filled the upper part of the lake bed, leaving Semerwater – at half a mile (800m) long Yorkshire's largest natural lake.

### Legendary Semerwater

Semerwater boasts several legends. One concerns the three huge blocks of limestone deposited by the departing glacier at the water's edge at the north end. Called the Carlow Stone and the Mermaid Stones, they are said to have landed here when the Devil and a giant who lived on Addlebrough, the prominent hill a mile (1.6km) to the east, began lobbing missiles at each other. More famous is the story of the beggar who came to the town that once stood where the lake is now. He went from door to door, asking for food and drink, but was refused by everyone – except the poorest couple. Revealing himself as an angel, he raised his staff over the town, crying 'Semerwater rise, Semerwater sink, And swallow all save this little house, That gave me meat and drink.' The waters overwhelmed the town, leaving the poor people's cottage on the brink of the new lake. Some say the church bells can still be heard ringing beneath the waters.

### Behind the Legend

There are indeed the remains of a settlement beneath Semerwater. Houses perched on stilts were built along the water's edge in Iron Age times, though there may have been an earlier settlement here in Neolithic times, too, for flint arrow heads have been found. A Bronze age spear head was found in 1937 when the lake's waters were lowered.

## Setts and Quakers

Marsett, at the lake's southern end, and Countersett, to the north, both end with the Old Norse word denoting a place of hill pasture. Marsett is a hamlet of old farmhouses, and on the road to Countersett, at Carr End, is the house where Dr Fothergill was born in 1712. A famous Quaker philanthropist, he founded the Quaker school at Ackworth in South Yorkshire. The American statesman Benjamin Franklin said he found it hard to believe that any better man than Fothergill had ever lived. Countersett has one of several old Friends' Meeting Houses in Wensleydale, and the Hall was home, in the 17th century, to Richard Robinson, who was responsible for the spread of Quakerism in the Dales.

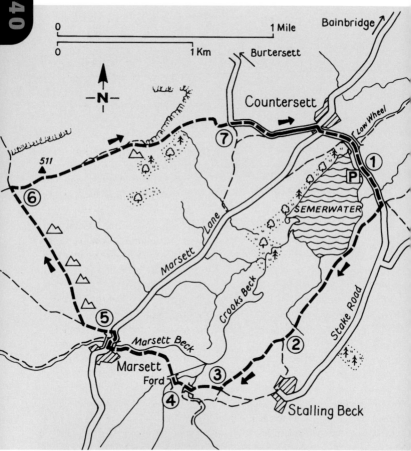

## Walk 40 Directions

① Turn right out of the car park up the road. Opposite farm buildings go right over a ladder stile, signed 'Stalling Busk'. Go through a gated stile and ahead towards the barn, then through two stone stiles. Just beyond the second is a Wildlife Trust sign. Continue over two more stiles to a gate.

② Just beyond the gate, follow the **Marsett** sign to the corner of the field and over a gated stone stile. Follow the waymarked path as it curves beside the river, to a barn.

Walk 40

Go over a stile above the barn to another stile. Cross the field to another stile and on towards another barn, and on further to cross a stream bed.

③ Immediately afterwards, turn right down the well-worn footpath, which curves towards a roofless barn. Cross another three stiles, then turn right, following a path to the trees, with a stone wall on your right. Continue over two stiles to a footbridge and go straight on to a track, where you turn right to reach a ford.

**WHAT TO LOOK FOR** ⓘ

Semerwater offers a wide variety of habitats for wildlife. The waters of the lake, which have a high plankton content, support many fish including bream and perch, as well as crayfish. Water birds include great crested grebe and tufted duck. You may also occasionally see Whooper swans. Over the fringes of the lake dragonflies and damsel flies can be seen glittering in the summer. On the wet margins of the lake grow flowers such as marsh marigold, marsh cinquefoil, ragged robin and valerian, while in the dryer areas the wood anemone is frequently found. Birds such as lapwings, redshank and reed bunting may also be seen, while summer visitors include the sandmartin.

④ Before the ford, veer left over a footbridge and back on to the track, which winds into **Marsett**. Just before the village, follow the stream as it goes right, and make for the road by the red telephone box. Turn right over the bridge. 100yds (91m) beyond take a track signed **Burtersett and Hawes** (not the path by the river).

**WHILE YOU'RE THERE** ⓘ

Visit **Bainbridge**, with its wide green and attractive houses. The Romans had a fort here, Virosidum, on top of the hill called Brough. The River Bain, crossed by the bridge which gives the village its name, is England's shortest river, running all of 2 miles (3.2km) from Semerwater to the River Ure.

⑤ Walk uphill to a gate on the right at the start of the stone wall. Go over the stile and continue uphill, over three stiles. Soon after the steep path flattens out, you reach a track that crosses the path, coming through a gap in the wall on your left.

⑥ Turn right along the track, which goes through a gate in a wall. Where it divides, take the right fork downhill to a stile. The path descends steeply through two gates, to reach a crossing track. Continue straight ahead and follow the track as it bends left to a gate on to a metalled road.

⑦ Turn right and follow the road downhill to the staggered crossroads, turning right, then left, signed '**Stalling Busk**'. Go down the hill, over the bridge and back to the car park.

**WHERE TO EAT AND DRINK** ⓘ

The nearest place to Semerwater is Bainbridge, where the **Rose and Crown Hotel** by the Green dates back more than 500 years. The Bainbridge Horn, blown to guide travellers to the village in the dark winter months, hangs here. The hotel serves home-cooked local produce both in the bars and, in the evening, in the Dales Room Restaurant.

# Four Seasons by Elter Water and Loughrigg Tarn

*Bluebell woods, a lake, a tarn, a waterfall and Little Loughrigg, make this a memorable outing.*

**Walk 41**

| | |
|---|---|
| •DISTANCE• | 4 miles (6.4km) |
| •MINIMUM TIME• | 2hrs |
| •ASCENT / GRADIENT• | 328ft (100m) ▲▲▲ |
| •LEVEL OF DIFFICULTY• | 🚶🚶 🚶🚶 🚶 |
| •PATHS• | Grassy and stony paths and tracks, surfaced lane, 4 stiles |
| •LANDSCAPE• | Lake, tarn, fields, woods, open fellside, views to fells |
| •SUGGESTED MAP• | aqua3 OS Explorer OL 7 The English Lakes (SE) |
| •START / FINISH• | Grid reference: NY 328048 |
| •DOG FRIENDLINESS• | Under control at all time; fellside grazed by sheep |
| •PARKING• | National Trust pay-and-display car park at Elterwater village |
| •PUBLIC TOILETS• | Above car park in Elterwater village |

## BACKGROUND TO THE WALK

Although it does include steep sections of ascent and descent this is not a desperately difficult walk. There are outstanding views throughout its length. The little lake of Elter Water and the petite Loughrigg Tarn are amongst the prettiest stretches of water in the region. The former, really three interconnected basins, was originally named Eltermere, which translates directly from the Old Norse (Viking) into 'swan lake'. The swans are still here in abundance. Be careful they don't grab your sandwiches should you choose to eat your lunch sat on the wooden bench at the foot of the lake. The views over both lake and tarn, to the reclining lion profile of the Langdale Pikes are particularly evocative.

Each season paints a different picture. Golden daffodils by Langdale Beck in early spring, bluebells in Rob Rash woods in May, yellow maple in Elterwater village in October and a thousand shades of green, everywhere, all summer. The river is dominant throughout the lower stages of the walk. It starts as the Great Langdale Beck, before emerging from the confines of Elter Water as the sedate River Brathay. Ascent then leads to the suspended bowl of Loughrigg Tarn, followed by the open fell freedom of Little Loughrigg. This is very much a walk for all seasons, and should the section through the meadows by the Brathay be flooded, then a simple detour can easily be made on to the road to bypass the problem.

### Local Gunpowder Works

With all the quarrying and mining that once took place in the Lake District, not to mention a little poaching for the pot, there used to be a considerable demand for 'black powder' or gunpowder, as it is more commonly known. Without treason or plot, Elterwater Gunpowder works, founded in 1824, once filled that demand. The natural water power of Langdale Beck was utilised to drive great grinding wheels or millstones. Prime quality charcoal came from the local coppices, whilst saltpetre and sulphur were imported. In the 1890s the works employed around 80 people. Accidental explosions did occur, notably in 1916 when four men were killed. The whole enterprise closed down in 1929. Today the site is occupied by the highly desirable Langdale Timeshare organisation, with only the massive mill wheels on display to bear witness to times past.

Of course, the raw ingredients had to be brought in and the highly explosive gunpowder taken away. That was done by horse and cart. My grandfather, Tommy Birkett, used to tend and groom the cart horses. Clydesdales were preferred for their huge strength and considerable intelligence. On workdays he would harness them up and on special occasions they had their mains plaited and ribboned and they were decorated with polished horse brasses. The horses have long gone but some of their brasses remain fixed to the oak beams in the Brittania Inn. Some I keep in my studio in Little Langdale.

## Walk 41 **Directions**

① Pass through a small gate to walk downsteam above **Great Langdale Beck**. Continue to enter the mixed woods of **Rob Rash**. A little gate leads through the stone wall, the open foot of **Elter Water** lies to the right. Continue along the path through the meadows above the river. This section can be wet and is prone to flooding. Pass through the gate and enter mixed woods. Keep along the path to pass **Skelwith Force** waterfall down to the right.

Walk 41

A little bridge leads across a channel to a viewing point above the falls. Keep along the path to pass through industrial buildings belonging to **Kirkstone Quarry**.

② **Kirkstone Gallery** is on the right, as the path becomes a small surfaced road. Continue to intercept the **A593** by the bridge over the river where there are picnic benches. Turn left to pass the hotel. At the road junction, cross directly over the Great Langdale road to gain a lane which passes by the end of the cottages. Follow the lane, ascending to intercept another road. Turn right for a short distance and then left towards **Tarn Foot** farm. Bear right along the track, in front of the row of cottages. Where the track splits, bear left. Through the gate continue along the track to overlook **Loughrigg Tarn**. At a point half-way along the tarn cross the stile over the iron railings on the left.

③ Follow the footpath down the meadow to traverse right, just above the tarn. The footpath swings off right to climb a ladder stile over the

stone wall. Follow the grassy track leading right, up the hill, to a gate and stile on to the road. Turn left along the road, until a surfaced drive leads up to the right, signed 'Public Footpath Skelwith Bridge'. Pass a small cottage and keep on the track to pass a higher cottage, **Crag Head**. A little way above this, a narrow grassy footpath leads off right, up the hillside, to gain a level shoulder between the craggy outcrops of **Little Loughrigg**.

④ Cross the shoulder and descend the path, passing a little tarnlet to the right, to intercept a stone wall. Keep left along the wall descending to find, in a few hundred paces, a ladder stile leading over the wall into the upper woods of **Rob Rash**. A steep descent leads down to the road. Cross this directly, and go over the little stone stile/broken wall next to the large double gates. Descend a track to meet up with the outward route. Bear right to return to **Elterwater** village.

# Along Ullswater's Shore to Silver Point

*From the shores of Ullswater to one of its most spectacular viewpoints.*

| | |
|---|---|
| **•DISTANCE•** | 4 miles (6.4km) |
| **•MINIMUM TIME•** | 1hr 30min |
| **•ASCENT / GRADIENT•** | 490ft (150m) ▲▲▲ |
| **•LEVEL OF DIFFICULTY•** | 🚶 🚶 🚶 |
| **•PATHS•** | Stony tracks and paths, no stiles |
| **•LANDSCAPE•** | Lake and fell views, mixed woodland |
| **•SUGGESTED MAP•** | aqua3 OS Explorer OL 5 The English Lakes (NE) |
| **•START / FINISH•** | Grid reference: NY 396159 |
| **•DOG FRIENDLINESS•** | Passes through working farm and open hillside grazed by sheep, dogs must be under control at all times |
| **•PARKING•** | Fee car park opposite Patterdale Hotel |
| **•PUBLIC TOILETS•** | Opposite White Lion in Patterdale village centre |

## BACKGROUND TO THE WALK

The elongated hamlet of Patterdale has a rugged, mountain quality. Sited below the mighty Helvellyn massif its straggle of houses, inn, hotel, mountain rescue base, church and school have a certain bleakness about them. A perfect contrast to the splendour that is Ullswater, whose southern shore lies hardly a stone's throw away. This walk strolls through mixed woodland and open aspect above the shores of the lake to visit the famed viewpoint of Silver Point. The adventurous may also wish to make the scramble to the top of Silver Crag, as did horsedrawn coach parties of old, for an even better view over the lake.

### Ullswater

Undoubtedly one of the loveliest of the lakes, the three legs of Ullswater add up to a total length of 7½ miles (12.1km) with an average width of ½ mile (800m) and a maximum depth of 205ft (62.5m). It is Lakeland's second largest lake, not quite measuring up to Windermere. Its waters are exceptionally clear and in the deepest part of the lake, off Howtown, lives a curious fish called the schelly; a creature akin to a freshwater herring.

Apart from rescue and Park Ranger launches, you won't see many power boats here, but Ullswater 'Steamers' have three boats operating between Glenridding and Pooley Bridge during the summer. Alfred Wainwright (1907–91), known for his seven *Pictorial Guides to the Lakeland Fells*, regarded this to be a part of one of the most beautiful walks in the Lakes – a sentiment with which few would disagree. Preservation of the lake in its present form is due to a concerted campaign, led in Parliament by Lord Birkett, against the proposed Manchester Corporation Water Act in 1965. Although the act was passed, and water is extracted from the lake, the workings are hidden underground and designed in such a way as to make it impossible to lower the water level beyond the agreed limit.

Amongst the trees, beside the shore, it was the golden yellow daffodils of this lake that inspired William Wordsworth's most widely known poem, *I wandered lonely as a cloud* or *Daffodils* as it often referred to (published in 1807). His sister Dorothy recorded the event vividly in her diary: 'I never saw daffodils so beautiful. They grew among the mossy stones about and around them, some rested their heads upon these stones as on a pillar for weariness and the rest tossed and reeled and danced and seemed as if they verily laughed with the wind that blew them over the lake.' There is no doubt that this later helped William to pen his famous verse.

# Walk 42 Directions

① From the car park walk to the road and turn right towards the shore of **Ullswater**. Pass the school to a track leading off right, through the buildings. Follow the unsurfaced track over a bridge and continue to pass the stone buildings of **Side Farm** to join another unsurfaced track.

② Turn left along the undulating

**Walk 42**

track, with a stone wall to the left, and pass through mixed woodland, predominantly oak and ash, before open fellside appears above. Continue on through the campsite

---

### WHILE YOU'RE THERE    ⓘ

Take a look around the nearby village of **Glenridding**. It has an information centre, inns and a variety of shops and places of interest. It is now the main gateway to the high Helvellyn massif and a popular place for hillwalkers and climbers. Until the 1960s it was also an important mining village. The **Greenside Lead Mine**, located at the top of the valley, was the largest lead mine in Britain. All is now quiet, and a youth hostel occupies a former mine building.

---

to pass a stand of larch before descending to cross a little stream above the buildings of Blowick seen through the trees below. The path ascends again to crest a craggy knoll above the woods of **Devil's Chimney**. Make a steep descent following the path through the rocks (care required) before it levels to traverse beneath the craggy heights of **Silver Crag**. Caution is again needed as the steep ground falls directly to the lake below. A slight ascent, passing some fine holly trees, gains the shoulder of **Silver Point** and an outstanding view of Ullswater.

③ Follow the path, which sweeps beneath the end of Silver Crag and continue to pass a small stream before a steep stony path, eroded in places, breaks off to the right. Ascend this, climbing diagonally

---

### WHERE TO EAT AND DRINK    ⓘ

En route, **Side Farm** sometimes offers teas and ice creams and, in the centre of Patterdale, next to the road, stands the **White Lion Inn** which serves bar meals throughout the year.

---

right, through the juniper bushes. Gain the narrow gap which separates Silver Crag to the right from the main hillside of **Birk Fell** to the left. This little valley is quite boggy and holds a small tarnlet.

④ If you don't care for steep, exposed ground, follow the high narrow path to make a gradual descent south in the direction of Patterdale. But for those with a head for heights, a short steep scramble leads to the top of **Silver Crag** and a wonderful view. Care must be exercised for steep ground lies in all directions. Descend back to the ravine and the main path by the same route. The path is easy though it traverses the open fellside

---

### WHAT TO LOOK FOR    ⓘ

The distinctive golden yellow and white of the indigenous **daffodil** still abounds in the woods by the lake shore and may be seen at its best from mid-March to mid-April. This wild variety is smaller than the broader flowered cultivated version and, many would say, even more lovely. There has been concern recently that the introduction of cultivated daffodils to this area is actually damaging the survival prospects of its smaller relative and jeopardising the view Wordsworth loved.

---

and may be boggy in places. Pass open quarry workings, where there is a large unfenced hole next to the path (take care), and continue on, to cross over the slate scree of a larger quarry. Bear right to descend by a stream and cross a little footbridge leading to the gate at the end of a track.

⑤ Go left through the gate and follow the lane which leads through the meadows. Cross the bridge and join the road. Bear right through **Patterdale** to return to the car park.

# Keswick's Walla Crag Above Derwent Water

*Wonderful panoramas to the surrounding fells, a jewelled lake and sylvan splendour are the delights of this walk.*

| | |
|---|---|
| •DISTANCE• | 5¼ miles (8.4km) |
| •MINIMUM TIME• | 3hrs |
| •ASCENT / GRADIENT• | 1,083ft (330m) ▲▲▲ |
| •LEVEL OF DIFFICULTY• | 🚶 🚶 🚶 |
| •PATHS• | Good paths and tracks, steep ascent and descent, 3 stiles |
| •LANDSCAPE• | Woods, open fell and lakeside |
| •SUGGESTED MAP• | aqua3 OS Explorer OL 4 The English Lakes (NW) |
| •START / FINISH• | Grid reference: NY 265229 |
| •DOG FRIENDLINESS• | Fields and open fell grazed by sheep, open lakeside, suitable for dogs under control |
| •PARKING• | Derwent Head car park |
| •PUBLIC TOILETS• | At Derwent Head, above lake |

## BACKGROUND TO THE WALK

At the foot of Borrowdale, often referred to as the most beautiful valley in England, the northern head of Derwent Water opens to Keswick and the northern fells with dramatic effect. Whilst experiencing the considerable charm of the woods and lakeside, the highlight of this walk is undeniably the staggering view from the heights of Walla Crag. West across Derwent Water, beyond Cat Bells, Maiden Moor and the secretive Newland Valley, stand the striking north western fells of Causey Pike, Sail, Crag Hill and Grisedale Pike. To the south west rise Glaramara and Great Gable. To the north Skiddaw and Blencathra. Undeniably one of the most evocative viewpoints within the whole of the Lake District National Park.

**Tank Manoeuvres**

This walk touches the lake shore before traversing the oak woods of Cockshot and Castlehead, to rise to the craggy top of Castle Head. A fine viewpoint in its own right, guarded on three sides by steep crags, it is reputedly the site of an Iron-Age hill fort. Springs Wood follows before ascent can be made to the steep open shoulder leading to Walla Crag. The metal strips seen in the track once provided grip for the caterpillar tracks of tanks on training manoeuvres here during the Second World War. Before the latest metric surveys by the Ordnance Survey the height of Walla Crag was easy to remember – it was 1,234ft above sea level! Descent through Great Wood follows and a delectable stroll home along the shore of this beautiful lake.

**Derwent Water**

The lake is 3 miles (4.8km) long and 72ft (22m) deep and is fed by the River Derwent. A speed limit ensures that motor powered boats do not ply its waters. Seasonal salmon, brown trout, Arctic char, perch and the predatory pike swim beneath the surface.

There are four islands on the lake, all owned by the National Trust. The largest and most northerly of the four is Derwent Isle. Once owned by Fountains Abbey it was bought by German miners from the Company of Mines Royal in 1569. The island and part of its grand 18th-century house are open to visitors on a handful of days during the year. St Herbert's Island was reputedly home to the Christian missionary of that name in the 10th century and monks remained in residence after his departure. A ruinous summer house is all that stands there today.

By the path, just above Derwent Bay, is an inscribed slate plaque in honour of Canon H D Rawnsley who did much to keep the lake as it remains today. He was vicar of Crosthwaite, the parish church of Keswick, from 1883 to 1917, and was one of Lakeland's greatest conservationists. In 1895 he became a co-founder of the National Trust. He was a campaigner against rude postcards and also encouraged Beatrix Potter to publish her first book *The Tale of Peter Rabbit* in 1900.

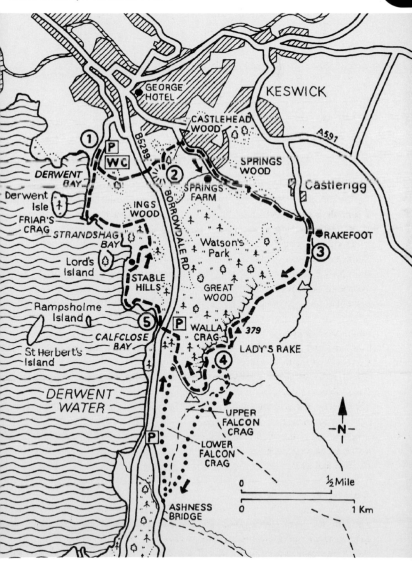

**Walk 43** *Directions*

Walk 43

① Proceed down the road to **Derwent Bay**. Go left opposite the landing stages, past the toilets, to take the track through **Cockshot Wood**. Walk through the wood and exit on to a fenced lane which leads across the field to the **Borrowdale road**. Cross the road and climb the stone steps to enter **Castlehead Wood**. Take the path which trends left to ascend the shoulder. In a little way a steeper path climbs up to the right, to the rocky summit of **Castle Head** and a fine viewpoint.

---

**WHAT TO LOOK FOR**  ⓘ

The rocky knoll of **Friar's Crag**, with its stand of Scots pine, is one of the most famous lakeside viewpoints. It is said to take its name from the friars who once lived on St Herbert's Island. At the foot of the crag, attached to the rocks which are often submerged when the lake level is high, memorial plaques detail all the former mayors of Keswick.

---

② Descend by the same route to reach the shoulder, then follow the path right to find a kissing gate. Exit the wood and enter a lane through the field. Continue to **Springs Road** and go right. Ascend to cross a bridge by **Springs Farm**. Take the track up through **Springs Wood**. Bear right at the junction then follow up the edge of the wood to pass the TV mast. Ascend until a footbridge crosses left to **Castlerigg Road**. Bear right and continue, to find a footbridge below **Rakefoot**.

③ Cross the footbridge over the stream. Turn left and follow the path, ascending by the stone wall. Cross a stile, and walk out on to the open shoulder of the fell, ascending the steep grassy nose. The going

levels until a stile on the right, through the fence line, leads to a path which follows the edge of the crag. Caution, there is a steep unfenced drop. Those wishing to stay away from the cliff edge can take a higher stile. Follow the path which crosses the head of a gully, **Lady's Rake**, to climb on to the polished rock cap of **Walla Crag** where the views are superb.

---

**WHERE TO EAT AND DRINK**  ⓘ

In Keswick you'll find the **George Hotel**, the town's oldest inn, which serves Jennings real ales and has both restaurant and bar meal facilities. There is also a **café** overlooking Derwent Bay.

---

④ Return to the boundary and follow the wall down, taking the lower stile. The path descends steeply above **Cat Gill**. Descend to a track by a bridge and bear right into **Great Wood**. Follow the track then descend left into the car park. Continue straight across, to find a path which descends to a gap in the wall by the **Borrowdale Road**. Take the gap in the wall opposite and follow the path to the lake shore.

⑤ Bear right, following around **Calfclose Bay**, by **Stable Hills**, around **Ings Wood** and **Strandshag Bay** to the Scots pine on **Friar's Crag**. Continue easily back to **Derwent Bay** and take the footpath along the road side to the car park.

---

**WHILE YOU'RE THERE**  ⓘ

The **Derwentwater Motor Launch Company** runs regular sailings both clockwise and anticlockwise around the lake. Landing stages en route include Ashness Gate, Lodore, High Brandlehow, Low Brandlehow, Hawes End and Nichol End. It makes for a good walk to take the boat out and return by foot to Keswick. Family tickets offer good value.

# Valley of the Shining Water

*Exploring one of Northumberland's most attractive river valleys.*

| | |
|---|---|
| **·DISTANCE·** | 3¾ miles (6km) |
| **·MINIMUM TIME·** | 2hrs 15min |
| **·ASCENT / GRADIENT·** | 590ft (180m) ▲▲▲ |
| **·LEVEL OF DIFFICULTY·** | 🚶 🚶 🚶 |
| **·PATHS·** | Good river paths and faint field paths, 19 stiles |
| **·LANDSCAPE·** | Riverside and high pasture |
| **·SUGGESTED MAP·** | aqua3 OS Explorer OL43 Hadrian's Wall |
| **·START / FINISH·** | Grid reference: NY 838558 |
| **·DOG FRIENDLINESS·** | Farming country, keep dogs on leads |
| **·PARKING·** | Ample parking in village centre |
| **·PUBLIC TOILETS·** | In village centre |

## BACKGROUND TO THE WALK

If you were dropped into East Allendale you could be forgiven for thinking you were in the northern part of the Yorkshire Dales. Like that area it's rugged rather than beautiful, but it's also peaceful and serene. Appropriately, Allen comes from the Celtic word 'aln' which means shining or foaming. The main centre, Allendale Town, is set on a hillside overlooking a bend in the East Allen River and sheltered beneath the heather moors of Hexhamshire Common. It proclaims itself to be the true geographical centre of Britain, and co-ordinates inscribed on to the church tower's sundial reinforce this.

### Mining Town

On entering the large Market Square with its many large hotels and inns, it soon becomes obvious that this place has seen busier times, and so it has. This was a mining town, the most prosperous in the whole of the region, with good veins of lead and silver. In the halcyon days of the 18th century Allendale had a population of over 5,500, four times what it is today. Allendale was lively, for the miners were hard-working, hard-drinking men who filled each and everyone of the inns. Even with the death of their industry at the turn of the century, the place stayed busy, with motor coaches bringing people from the industrial north east for health and enjoyment.

Perhaps Allendale is most famous for its Baal Fire Festival, which takes place each New Year's Eve. It's said to be of Viking origin. At 11:30PM the pubs empty and a crowd gathers in the square. Suddenly the night sky is lit up by a procession of 40 men dressed in fancy costumes and with flaming tar barrels on their heads. The men, known as guisers, parade around the town streets accompanied by the Allendale Silver Band. Close to midnight the guisers hurl the burning contents of the barrels on to a bonfire, whose flames then explode high into the sky. It's a dangerous procedure, usually resulting in a few singed eyebrows. The church bells chime in the New Year and everybody sings *Auld Lang Syne* before returning to the pub for more celebrations.

There are many long walks from Allendale Town to the moors but a good introduction explores the immediate environs of the valley itself. Passing the old inns you go down to the river, which is lined by fine stands of trees. In spring and early summer the fields and woods will be full of wild flowers like bloody cranesbill, wild primrose, herb Robert and ragwort.

Later the walk climbs away, to high fields and old farms looking down on the rooftops of Allendale Town. The river, in some places hidden by trees, but in others shining among the valley meadows, meanders into the distance to those dark North Pennine moors that yawn across the western skies.

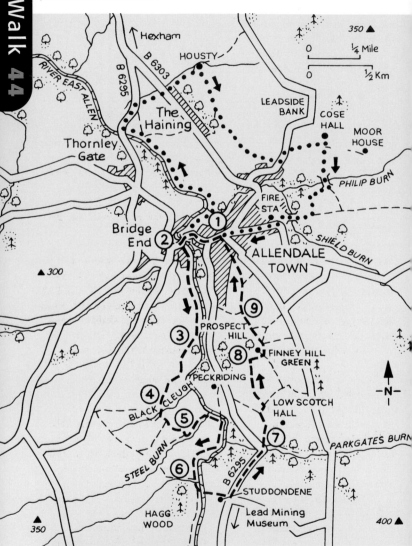

# Walk 44 Directions

① From the **Market Place** take the Whitfield road down past the **Hare and Hounds** and round the left-hand bend to the old **Mill Bridge** across the **River East Allen**.

② Immediately beyond the bridge, turn left along a tarred lane past some cottages – it's highlighted by a footpath sign 'to Wooley Scar'. Where the track swings right leave it and go through the gate ahead

Walk 44

before following a cross-field path, parallel to the river.

③ At the narrow end of a wedge shaped field go over a ladder stile on the right. Here the path veers away from the river and enters an area above **Wooley Scar**, which can be slightly overgrown with nettles and ragwort in the summer months. The route continues generally south west across fields.

④ Beyond **Black Cleugh** it swings south east along a short section of rutted track. Ignoring the first stile on the right follow the right field edge. A waymark on a broken fence points the way down towards the woods surrounding **Steel Burn**.

⑤ Turn left along a grass track running parallel to the burn and go through a gate behind a little cottage. Turn right over a footbridge crossing the burn, then follow the banks of the **East Allen**. The clear route crosses riverside

meadows and ignores the first river footbridge near **Peckriding**.

⑥ After meandering with the river, the path comes upon a track near **Hagg Wood** and follows it across a bridge over the East Allen. The track zig-zags past the farm at **Studdondene** to reach the **B6295** where you turn left.

⑦ On reaching the woods of **Parkgates Burn** take the left of two waymarked paths. Over a stile it climbs fields towards the left of two farmhouses on the skyline – **Low Scotch Hall**. It turns right then left to round the farmhouse, now following the left field edge high above the valley.

⑧ On reaching the woods of **Prospect Hill** turn right through some animal pens then along an enclosed path to the farm of **Finney Hill Green**. Turn left beyond the house and continue along the left edge of three fields.

⑨ A modern housing estate at the edge of **Allendale Town** comes into view and the path heads north, parallel to the houses. In the last field it descends towards some more mature housing and enters an estate through a little ginnel. Go past the children's playground and out on to the main road in the village centre.

# Around Druridge Bay

*A nature reserve, country park and beach, each with its own interest.*

| | |
|---|---|
| •DISTANCE• | 5½ miles (8.8km) |
| •MINIMUM TIME• | 1hr 45min |
| •ASCENT / GRADIENT• | Negligible |
| •LEVEL OF DIFFICULTY• | |
| •PATHS• | Paths and tracks, with good walk on beach, no stiles |
| •LANDSCAPE• | Dunes, seashore and lakeside |
| •SUGGESTED MAP• | aqua3 OS Explorers 325 Morpeth & Blyth; 332 Alnwick & Amble |
| •START / FINISH• | Grid reference: NU 282024 (on Explorer 332) |
| •DOG FRIENDLINESS• | On lead within nature reserve |
| •PARKING• | Car park at Hauxley Nature Reserve |
| •PUBLIC TOILETS• | At Hauxley Nature Reserve and Druridge Bay Country Park visitor centres |
| •NOTE• | Check tides; complete coastal section not always passable at high water |

## BACKGROUND TO THE WALK

The story of Druridge Bay's pools begins 300 millions years ago, when the area basked in a warm climate and was cloaked in a dense, forest swamp. The gradual accumulation of decaying vegetation eventually gave rise to extensive coal deposits, which today extend far out to sea. Although dug from shallow drifts or bell pits since the medieval period, it was only during the Industrial Revolution that coal mining began in earnest. Pits were sunk ever deeper, and mining developed as a major industry along the north east coast, with villages such as nearby Broomhill springing up to house miners and their families.

### Opencast Mining

As the 20th century progressed, many pits became worked out or uneconomic, yet with the Second World War, the need for coal had never been greater. A new approach was tried, with the country's first opencast operation beginning on Town Moor near Newcastle. Far cheaper and simpler than deep mining, the scale of workings steadily increased, as the equipment needed to excavate and move immense quantities of rock was improved.

Work began on the Radcliffe site in September 1971, and a staggering 100 million tons of overlying rock was removed to extract some 2½ million tons of coal. Within seven years, all the coal was out, leaving behind a crater 170ft (52m) deep. The Northumberland Wildlife Trust bought part of the site in 1983 and has turned the derelict wasteland into the nature-rich lakes and islands we see today.

### Nature Reserves

Hauxley Pool is typical of the several flooded workings along the coast, and although huge numbers of trees, shrubs and other plants were originally brought in, there is now a remarkably natural feel to the water and its surroundings. As the fertility of the once-barren land has been improved, many species have become established on the banks and, in spring and summer, the place is alive with colour from bloody cranesbill, yellow wort, kidney vetch and a host of other flowers. Look carefully and you'll spot the delicate pink petals of ragged robin, an often-rare sight in today's countryside.

The attraction for many visitors, however, is the variety and numbers of birds that visit these coastal lakes, a spectacle that is ever-changing throughout the year. Resident populations are joined by those migrating between the summer feeding and breeding grounds in the far north and the warmer climes of Africa, where many spend the winter. Dunlin, whimbrel and sanderling are amongst the many species passing through, whilst redshank, plover and bar-tailed godwit are some that winter here. You will also see whooper and Bewick swans as well as many favourites such as tits, finches, blackbirds and robins.

## Walk 45 **Directions**

① A waymarked footpath beside the car park entrance winds between the nature reserve and a caravan site towards the coast.

Through a gate at the bottom, turn right on to a track, which shortly passes two gates that give access to bird hides overlooking the lake.

② Leaving the reserve, continue a little further along a tarmac track to

**Walk 45**

an informal parking area on the left, where there is easy access on to the beach. Now, follow the shore past **Togston Links**, across a stream and on below **Hadston Links**.

③ After 1¼ miles (2km), wooden steps take the path off the sands on to the dunes. Cross a tarmac track and continue over a marshy area into pinewood. Beyond the trees, emerge by a car park and walk across to the **Druridge Bay Country Park visitor centre**, where there is a café and toilets.

④ A footway to the left winds around **Ladyburn Lake**, soon passing a boat launching area. Keep to the lower path, which soon leads to stepping stones across the upper neck of the lake. If you would rather not cross there, continue around the upper edge of a wooded nature sanctuary above the water to a footbridge higher up. Over the bridge and through a gate, turn right by the field edge, soon dropping around an internal corner to a kissing gate. Descend through trees to regain the lake by the stepping stones.

⑤ This side of the lake has a more 'natural' feel, the path winding through trees to emerge beside a lushly vegetated shoreline where swans like to feed. After crossing a bridge over the lake's outflow, carry on back to the visitor centre.

⑥ Retrace your steps to the beach and turn back towards **Hauxley**, but when you reach the point at which you originally dropped on to the sands, remain on the shore towards **Bondi Carrs**. Seaweed can make the rocks slippery, so be careful clambering over as you round the point, where Coquet Island then comes into view ahead. Not far beyond there, after passing a look-out post and approaching large rocks placed as a storm defence, leave across the dunes, retracing your outward path the short distance back to the car park.

### WHERE TO EAT AND DRINK ⓘ

If you're looking for refreshment during the walk, call in at the Druridge Bay Country Park **visitor centre**, where the café offers an appetising selection of snacks and light meals. However, for something more substantial, try the **Widdrington Inn**, which you'll find beside a roundabout on the A1068, about 4 miles (6.4km) to the south.

### WHAT TO LOOK FOR ⓘ

In many places, the base of the **dunes** overlooking the beach has eroded to give the appearance of low, crumbling cliffs. Look carefully and you will see that they are banded. At the base is sandstone bedrock, formed when the area was flooded some 250 million years ago, at the end of the Carboniferous period. Immediately above is boulder clay, a mere 10,000 years old, deposited by melting ice sheets, and overlying that is peat, laid down between 3,000 to 5,000 years ago when the area was marshy. The dunes themselves have accumulated since then, the product of wind-blown sand.

# The Solway Shore from Carsethorn to Arbigland

*Visit the birthplace of John Paul Jones, the 'father of the American Navy'.*

| | |
|---|---|
| •DISTANCE• | 5½ miles (8.8km) |
| •MINIMUM TIME• | 2hrs 30min |
| •ASCENT / GRADIENT• | 82ft (25m) ▲▲ ▲ ▲ |
| •LEVEL OF DIFFICULTY• | 👫 👫 👫 |
| •PATHS• | Rocky seashore, woodland tracks and country roads |
| •LANDSCAPE• | Seashore, woodland and pasture |
| •SUGGESTED MAP• | aqua3 OS Explorer 313 Dumfries & Dalbeattie, New Abbey |
| •START / FINISH• | Grid reference: NX 993598 |
| •DOG FRIENDLINESS• | Good walk for dogs |
| •PARKING• | Car park by beach at Carsethorn |
| •PUBLIC TOILETS• | At John Paul Jones Museum |

## BACKGROUND TO THE WALK

The man hailed in the USA as the 'father of the American Navy' was born John Paul in a poor gardener's cottage at Arbigland, on the Solway coast in 1745.

### Young Seaman

At the age of 13 John signed up as an apprentice seaman journeying to Virginia on the *Friendship of Whitehaven*. He later signed on as third mate on a slave ship, the *King George of Whitehaven*. He lasted two years and advanced to first mate before he quit in disgust with the slave trade. On his passage home he acquired his first command when the captain and mate of his vessel died of fever. As the only qualified man left, John took control and brought the ship safely home. The owners rewarded him with permanent command. He had a reputation for a fiery temper and was once charged with murder but found not guilty. In 1773 he fled the West Indies, after killing the ringleader of a mutiny, and went to Virginia. It was around this time that he changed his name to John Paul Jones.

### American Naval Officer

In the lead up to the American Revolution (War of American Independence) when Congress was forming a 'Continental Navy', Jones offered his services and was commissioned as a first lieutenant on the *Alfred* in 1775. Later, as captain of the *Providence*, he advised Congress on naval regulations. In 1778, after a daring hit-and-run raid on Whitehaven, he sailed across the Solway to Kirkcudbright Bay to kidnap the Earl of Selkirk and ransom him for American captives. However the earl was not at home and the raiding party had to be content with looting the family silver.

### Famous Battle

In September 1779, as commodore of a small squadron of French ships, John Paul Jones engaged his ship the *Bonhomme Richard* with the superior HMS *Serapis* and HMS *Countess of Scarborough* off Flamborough Head. After a dreadful 4-hour fight, in which Jones was injured and his ship sunk, he eventually won the battle, transferred his crew to the *Serapis* and sailed for Holland with his prisoners and booty.

John Paul Jones died in France in 1792 and his body lay in an unmarked grave for over a century. His remains were eventually taken back to the USA amid great ceremony and he was finally laid to rest in the chapel crypt of the Annapolis Naval Academy in 1913.

## Walk 46 Directions

① From the car park at **Carsethorn** head down on to the beach and turn right. Continue walking along the shore for approximately 2 miles (3.2km). The beach at this point is sandy and may be strewn with driftwood, but if the tide is in you will be walking over more rocky ground.

② After you reach **The House on**

**the Shore**, which is beside the beach on your right, the headland juts out and you should look for a track heading uphill on the right. At the top of the hill a well-defined track heads alongside a stone wall.

> **WHERE TO EAT AND DRINK** ℹ️
>
> The **Steamboat Inn**, just opposite the car park at Carsethorn has been trading since 1813 and, while offering up-to-the-minute comforts, still retains the atmosphere of those bygone days when immigrants left here to take the steamer to Liverpool for onward transport to the colonies. A real fire, real ales and a reputation for the best food in the district makes this a natural choice for walkers and families.

③ Look for a fainter track leading off to the left, which descends steeply to arrive at the beach beside a natural rock arch called the **Thirl Stane**. You can go through the arch to the sea if the tide is in, although if the tide is out on this part of the coast, the sea will be far off in the distance.

④ Continue from here along the rocks on the pebble shore and up a grassy bank until you reach a car park. Exit the car park on to a lane. Continue on the lane past **Powillimount**. Turn right when you get to a lodge house on the right-hand side and walk along the estate road to reach the cottage birthplace of John Paul Jones.

⑤ There are picnic tables here and a fascinating small **museum**. Continue along the road past the gates to **Arbigland** on to the road signed 'No vehicular traffic'. Follow the road as it turns right and along the side of some of the Arbigland Estate buildings.

⑥ When the road turns left at a cottage, go right on to a dirt track. Follow the dirt track until it emerges on to a surfaced road next to **Tallowquhairn** to your right. Take the road away from the farm, turning sharply left around some houses, then right and continue to a T-junction.

⑦ Turn right and follow this road round to the left. Follow the long straight road as far as the right turn to **South Carse**. Go along the farm road and straight through the farm steading as far as you can go, then turn left.

> **WHAT TO LOOK FOR** ℹ️
>
> The rocks between Hogus Point and Arbigland date from the Carboniferous era some 345 million years ago. Fossils in this area are well exposed and those of coral, cuttlefish, fish vertebrae, shells and tooth plates can be found. Near the beach at Powillimount look for fossilised tree ferns.

⑧ To return to the shore again, walk along a footpath passing a brightly coloured caravan and the rear of some cottages. Look out for a narrow track heading downhill to the right allowing access to the beach. Turn left and walk along the beach to the car park.

> **WHILE YOU'RE THERE** ℹ️
>
> The Victorian **Shambellie House**, just outside the village of New Abbey, contains a unique collection of costumes and is part of the National Museums of Scotland. Most of the clothes are displayed in natural settings in a series of tableaux. In the dining room is an after dinner game of carpet bowls c1905 while two women in 1920s evening dress are playing the gramophone in the library and a 1930s bride is getting dressed in the bedroom.

# The Spectacular Falls at Glenashdale

*Enjoy this short scenic woodland walk over the Isle of Arran's ancient bedrock.*

| | |
|---|---|
| •DISTANCE• | 2¾ miles (4.4km) |
| •MINIMUM TIME• | 2hrs |
| •ASCENT / GRADIENT• | 442ft (135m) ▲▲▲ |
| •LEVEL OF DIFFICULTY• | 👫 👫 👫 |
| •PATHS• | Forest paths and forest roads |
| •LANDSCAPE• | Woodland, waterfalls, rock |
| •SUGGESTED MAP• | aqua3 OS Explorer 361 Isle of Arran |
| •START / FINISH• | Grid reference: NS 047252 |
| •DOG FRIENDLINESS• | Good, locals walk their dogs here |
| •PARKING• | Car park opposite youth hostel in Whiting Bay |
| •PUBLIC TOILETS• | None on route; nearest at Shore Road, Whiting Bay |

## BACKGROUND TO THE WALK

Millions of years ago this area was a hot and barren desert. During what geologists refer to as the Permian period, 270 million years ago, the underlying red sandstone gradually formed from sand dunes. On top of this a sill (layer) of igneous rocks was laid down in the Tertiary period 210 million years later.

### The Glenashdale Sill

The Tertiary sill at Glenashdale is about 100ft (30m) thick and composed of several types of igneous rock, the major part being quartz-dolerite. When this is harder than the surrounding rock, it stands proud as the softer rocks are eroded. At Glenashdale continual erosion has created these spectacular waterfalls and, where the stream and the waterfall have cut into the Glenashdale sill, it is easy to examine the now exposed structure of the rocks. Following the stream up from the waterfall the banks and bed of the stream reveal the dark and medium grained igneous rocks with a few specks of pyrites – a shiny yellow mineral. South west of the falls there are veins of a dark basalt. Pack one of those small geological field guides in your backpack, or in a pocket, and use the photographs to help identify the various different kinds of rock found on the route.

### Native and Exotic Trees

A field guide to trees could also prove useful although several of the trees have been conveniently labelled. There is an abundance of native trees like the alder, hazel, downy birch, oak, ash and rowan. The latter, also called the mountain ash, has bright red berries in the autumn and in Scottish folklore was used for warding off witches.

You'll also find a wide variety of unusual and exotic trees in the glen. The Siberian crab has white flowers and small green berries which may eventually turn into bright red fruits. You'll also come across large specimens of the Douglas fir. This evergreen native of North America is extensively planted in Europe to provide high grade timber but seldom reaches its maximum height of 328ft (100m). Most European specimens tend to be around 180ft (55m). Other North American species include the Great fir and the Sitka spruce. This fast growing conifer often reaches heights of 197ft (60m) and although it thrives in a range of soils, it is particularly suited to the mild, wet Scottish climate.

Growing on the edge of the path you'll find the heart shaped leaves of wood sorrel with its long stalked, white, bell-like flowers during April and May. There's a profusion of red campion and the scent of wild honeysuckle and pungent wild garlic mingle with the pine tang of the wood. If you look really hard you may even find a yellow pimpernel, with its star-like flowers, in May and August.

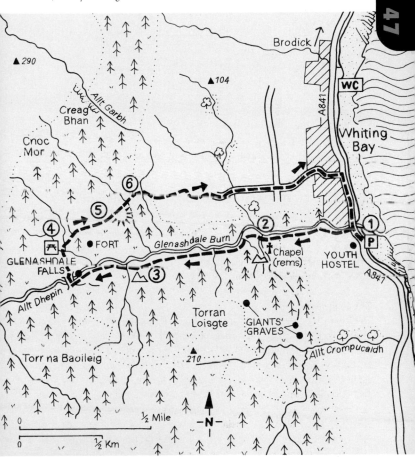

# Walk 47 **Directions**

① From the car park turn right on to the road, cross it and turn left on to the footpath, signposted 'Giants' Graves and Glenashdale Falls'. Follow this leafy lane until it reaches the rear of a house, then continue on the path along the riverbank. Go through a gate, pass a forest walks sign and continue until you reach a signpost pointing in the direction of the **Giants' Graves**.

② The path forks here. Go right, following the sign to **Glenashdale Falls**. The path continues, rising gently, through a wooded area, where several of the trees are identified by small labels fixed to the trunks. Continue uphill on this path, which is marked by the occasional waymarker, crossing several bridges and fording a shallow section of the burn.

③ Eventually the path starts to climb steeply uphill and continues to some steps and then forks. Keep right and follow this path to reach the falls. Keep on the path past the falls and continue uphill to cross a bridge. A picnic table situated on the riverbank here is a good spot to stop for refreshment.

---

### WHERE TO EAT AND DRINK ⓘ

There are plenty of choices for eating and drinking in Whiting Bay. **The Pantry** on Shore Road is open every day until 9PM in the summer, with restricted hours from November. The **Trafalgar Restaurant**, also on Shore Road, serves a variety of main meals and snacks while the **Drift Inn**, just off Shore Road by Murchies, does superb bar food.

---

④ From here follow the path into an area planted with Sitka spruce. Keep to the track marked by the green waymarkers as it heads through this dark part, going through a gap in a wall and eventually arriving at a sign pointing to an **Iron-Age fort**. Turn off to look at the remains of the ramparts then retrace your steps to the sign and continue on the path.

---

### WHAT TO LOOK FOR ⓘ

If you turn left at the sign for the Giants' Graves you can see the remains of **Whiting Bay Chapel**. In 20yds (18m) on the left look for a raised area covered with vegetation and poke about at the far end. Little remains but you should find some small gravestones.

---

⑤ Cross a bridge by another waterfall then follow more waymarkers to a clearing and a viewpoint. Sit on the bench here and enjoy the panoramic view across the wooded glen. From here you can see the full extent of the Glenashdale Falls as the water cascades over the top. A waymarker points uphill through a densely wooded area before ending at a T-junction with a forest road.

---

### WHILE YOU'RE THERE ⓘ

Visit the **Giants' Graves**, an important neolithic site containing several chambered burial cairns of the kind found throughout Arran. Because of their semi-circular forecourts they have been called 'horned gallery graves'. The path to the graves is short but steep, climbing some 173 steps.

---

⑥ Turn right on to the forest road and continue, crossing water at a ford and going through three kissing gates until the route continues as a metalled road. Continue along this, go over a crossroads and wind downhill. Turn right at a T-junction and walk 200yds (183m) back to the car park.

# The Shores of Loch Katrine

*Glasgow's water supply in the heart of the Trossachs.*

| | |
|---|---|
| **•DISTANCE•** | 6¾ miles (10.9km) |
| **•MINIMUM TIME•** | 4hrs 30min |
| **•ASCENT / GRADIENT•** | 420ft (128m) ▲▲ ▲ |
| **•LEVEL OF DIFFICULTY•** | 🚶 🚶 🚶 |
| **•PATHS•** | Water board roads, hill tracks |
| **•LANDSCAPE•** | Hills, woodland, lochs and heather |
| **•SUGGESTED MAP•** | aqua3 OS Explorers 364 Loch Lomond North; 365 The Trossachs |
| **•START / FINISH•** | Grid reference: NN 404102 (on Explorer 364) |
| **•DOG FRIENDLINESS•** | Keep on lead near loch and livestock |
| **•PARKING•** | Car park at Stronachlachar Pier |
| **•PUBLIC TOILETS•** | At car park |

## BACKGROUND TO THE WALK

Loch Katrine takes its name from the Gaelic 'cateran', a Highland robber – a fitting place then for the birthplace of Rob Roy MacGregor, the bandit, who was born at Glengyle at the western end of the loch. This is the heart of MacGregor country and one of their clan graveyards lies near the head of the loch. Rob Roy's lasting fame is due to a novel of the same name written by Sir Walter Scott and the loch, too, owed its early popularity to one of Scott's poems, *The Lady of the Lake*. First published in 1810, Scott's description of the dramatic scenery encouraged tourists to visit the Trossachs. The poets Coleridge and Wordsworth were inspired by its beauty and Queen Victoria enjoyed a leisurely sail upon the loch in 1869. But the pure water of the loch was destined to be a crucial element in the growth of the City of Glasgow as well as a rural escape for its citizens.

By the start of the 19th century Glasgow's population of over 80,000, depended for their drinking water on a few public wells. Later, private companies supplied water from large barrels, selling it from the back of horse-drawn wagons. But the poor quality of the water, combined with dreadful overcrowding and poor sanitation, led to thousands of deaths from cholera in the 1830s and 40s.

By the mid-19th century Glasgow resolved to provide a municipal waterworks and commissioned John Frederick Bateman, an English engineer. Bateman identified Loch Katrine as the best source of water for Glasgow because of the quality of the water, the large catchment area and its remote, rural, location, but it required a massive feat of engineering. Bateman first built a large dam to raise the level of the loch. Then he constructed an aqueduct, 26 miles (41.8km) long to transport the water to a huge reservoir at Mugdock, on the outskirts of the city. A further 26 miles (41.8km) of main piping and 46 miles (74km) of distribution pipes were installed to take the water to all quarters of Glasgow.

After three and a half years of constant work, this marvel of engineering was officially opened by Queen Victoria in October 1859. Bateman himself was mightily impressed by his scheme and told the city fathers that he had left them 'a work which I believe will, with very slight attention, remain perfect for ages, which for the greater part of it, is indestructible as the hills through which it has been carried.'

Walk 48

Stronachlachar
Eilean Dharag
PIER
P WC
LOCH KATRINE
Aqueduct
Outlet
B829
LOCH
ARKLET
ROYAL
COTTAGE
▲ 265
OBELISK
SHAFT
LOCH
ARD
FOREST
▲ 392
Lochan
Mhaim
nan Carn
FRENICH
FARM
Culligart Burn
B829
▲ 324
▲ 420
SHAFT
LOCH
CHON
IS
P
SHAFTS
▲ 508
Lochan
Beinn Dubh
▲ 482
Duchray Water
SHAFT
LOCH
DHU
LOCH DHU HOUSE
B8
SHAFT
Queen Elizabeth Forest Park
Aberfoy

-N-

0     ½ Mile
0     ½ Km

## Walk 48 **Directions**

① From the car park follow the road back towards the **B829** and take the second turning on the left. This is an access road for Scottish Water vehicles only. Continue along the access road until you come to a cattle grid with green gate posts at the building known as **Royal Cottage**. Turn right just before this on to a rough gravel track that heads through some dense bracken.

---

**WHAT TO LOOK FOR** ⓘ

Just off the pier at Stronachlacher is **Eilean Dharag**, a small wooded island where Rob Roy MacGregor reputedly incarcerated Graham of Killearn, the Duke of Montrose's factor. Rob Roy had also taken the opportunity to relieve Graham of the rents he had been collecting for his master. Graham of Killearn succeeded in escaping, but not until Rob Roy was far away.

---

② As the path emerges on to open hillside you will see the first of several ventilation shafts and beyond it, on the hill, a strange obelisk. Follow the path along this line. When you reach the **obelisk** be sure to look back for a super view over Loch Katrine below and across to the hills with their narrow passes where Rob Roy and his men moved from Loch Katrine to Balquhidder and beyond, moving cattle or

---

**WHERE TO EAT AND DRINK** ⓘ

This is one of those occasions where a **picnic** is the only practical option. There are lots of excellent spots on the route to sit down, pour a cup of hot soup from your flask and enjoy your sandwiches while you gaze in awe at the scenery. Alternatively head back into Aberfoyle to the **Forth Inn** next to the car park there.

---

escaping from the forces of law and order. Continue following the line of the ventilation shafts towards a chimney-like structure on top of a hill. From here go right and downhill. Take great care on this section as the path has eroded and is very steep. At the bottom, go through the gap at the junction of two fences. From here go left.

③ Follow a well-defined track that goes through some pine trees and past another ventilation shaft. Keep left at the shaft. It can be very muddy on this short stretch. Continue on the path until it intersects a forest road by a stream. Cross the road and look for a faint track continuing downhill in the same direction. In summer this path may be difficult to find because it's hidden by bracken. In this case follow the line of the telephone poles. Eventually after working downhill through more woodland the track emerges on to the **B829**.

---

**WHILE YOU'RE THERE** ⓘ

Head round to the Trossachs Pier and take a trip on the **SS *Sir Walter Scott***, the last of the screw-driven steamships in service on Scotland's inland waters. The trip sails via Stronachlachar and passes Royal Cottage, Ellen's Isle, the Factor's Island and Rob Roy's birthplace at Glelengyle House.

---

④ Turn right here and follow the road. It will eventually emerge from **Loch Ard Forest** into open countryside. Loch Arklet can be seen on the left; it is now connected to Loch Katrine by an underground pipeline. When the road reaches a T-junction with the Inversnaid road, turn right. When this road forks, turn right again and return to **Stronachlachar Pier**.

**Walk 49**

# The Braes o' Killiecrankie

*A deeply wooded riverside leads from the famous battlefield to Loch Faskally.*

| | |
|---|---|
| •DISTANCE• | 8¾ miles (14.1km) |
| •MINIMUM TIME• | 4hrs |
| •ASCENT / GRADIENT• | 492ft (150m) ▲▲ ▲ ▲ |
| •LEVEL OF DIFFICULTY• | 徒 徒 徒 |
| •PATHS• | Wide riverside paths, minor road, no stiles |
| •LANDSCAPE• | Oakwoods on banks of two rivers |
| •SUGGESTED MAP• | aqua3 OS Explorer 386 Pitlochry & Loch Tummel |
| •START / FINISH• | Grid reference: NN 917626 |
| •DOG FRIENDLINESS• | Off leads on riverside paths |
| •PARKING• | Killiecrankie visitor centre |
| •PUBLIC TOILETS• | At start |

## BACKGROUND TO THE WALK

> *'If ye'd hae been where I hae been*
> *Ye wouldna been sae swanky o*
> *If ye'd hae seen where I hae seen*
> *On the braes o Killiecrankie o'*

The song commemorating the victory of the Battle of Killiecrankie in July 1689 is still sung wherever anyone with an accordion sits down in a pub full of patriotic tourists. In fact, both sides in the battle were Scots. When James II was ousted from England in a bloodless coup in 1688, the Scots Parliament (the Estates) voted to replace him with William of Orange. The Stuarts had neglected and mismanaged Scotland, and had mounted a bloody persecution of the fundamentalist Protestants (Covenanters) of the Southern Uplands.

### 'Bluidy Clavers'

John Claverhouse, 'Bonnie Dundee', had earned the rather different nickname 'Bluidy Clavers' in those persecutions. He now raised a small army of Highlanders in support of King James. The Estates sent a larger army north under another Highlander, General Hugh Mackay, to sort things out. Dundee, outnumbered two to one, was urged to ambush Mackay in the Pass of Killiecrankie. He refused, on the grounds of chivalry. The path above the river was steep, muddy and wide enough for only two soldiers; a surprise attack on such difficult ground would give his broadsword-wielding Highlanders too great an advantage against Mackay's inexperienced troops. Just one of the Lowlanders was picked off by an Atholl sharpshooter at the Trouper's Den (below today's visitor centre), and the battle actually took place on open ground, to the north of the pass.

### Claymore Victorious

Killiecrankie was the last time the claymore conquered the musket in open battle, and it was down to a deficiency in the musket. Some 900 of the 2,500 Highlanders were shot down as they charged, but then the troopers had to stop to fix their bayonets, which plugged into the muzzle of the musket. By this time the Highlanders were upon them, and they broke and fled. The battle had lasted just three minutes. Half of Mackay's army was killed, wounded, captured or drowned in the Garry. One escaped by leaping 18ft (5.5m) across the river; the 'Soldier's Leap' is near the start of the walk. But the victory led nowhere. Bonnie Dundee died in the battle. A month later his army was defeated at Dunkeld, and 25 years later, when the Highlanders next brought their broadswords south for the Stuarts, the troopers had learnt to fix a bayonet to the side of a musket where it no longer blocked the barrel.

## Walk 49 Directions

① Cross the front of the visitor centre to steps, signed 'Soldier's Leap', leading down into the wooded gorge. A footbridge crosses

the waterfall of **Troopers' Den**. At the next junction, turn left ('Soldier's Leap'). Ten steps down, a spur path on the right leads to the viewpoint above the **Soldier's Leap**.

② Return to the main path, signed

'Linn of Tummel', which runs down to join the **River Garry** below the railway viaduct. After a mile (1.6km) it reaches a footbridge.

> **WHILE YOU'RE THERE** ⓘ
>
> At the Pitlochry dam that forms Loch Faskally, Scottish and Southern Energy has a small **visitor centre** celebrating its hydro-electric schemes. It also has a window into the salmon ladder beside the dam. From March to October you can watch the fish battle their way up towards Killiecrankie.

③ Don't cross this footbridge, but continue ahead, signed 'Pitlochry', along the riverside under the tall South Garry road bridge. The path runs around a huge river pool to a tarred lane; turn right here. The lane leaves the lochside, then passes a track on the right, blocked by a vehicle barrier. Ignore this; shortly turn right at a signpost, 'Pitlochry'.

④ Immediately bear left to pass along the right-hand side of **Loch Dunmore**, following red-top posts. A footbridge crosses the loch, but turn away from it, half right, on to a small path that becomes a dirt track. After 110yds (100m) it reaches a wider track. Turn left, with a white/yellow waymarker. After 220yds (201m) the track starts to climb; here the white/yellow markers indicate a smaller path on the right, which follows the lochside. Where it rejoins the wider path, bear right at a green

waymarker and cross a footbridge to the **A9** road bridge.

⑤ Cross **Loch Faskally** on the Clunie footbridge below the road's bridge and turn right, on to a quiet road around the loch. In 1 mile (1.6km), at the top of the grass bank on the left, is the **Priest Stone**. After the **Clunie power station**, you reach a car park on the left. Here a sign indicates a steep little path down to the **Linn of Tummel**.

> **WHERE TO EAT AND DRINK** ⓘ
>
> There are **cafés** at the start and at Lochside, Pitlochry. Pitlochry itself is the town of the tea room. One of them is **Macdonald's**, on the main street. You can get good bar meals at the **Old Mill Inn**, which also offers 100 malt whiskies and a waterwheel (children welcome; dogs in the outside seating area only).

⑥ Return to the road above for ½ mile (800m), to cross a grey suspension bridge on the right. Turn right, downstream, to pass above the **Linn**. A spur path back right returns to the falls at a lower level, but the main path continues along the riverside (signed 'Killiecrankie'). It bends left and goes down wooden steps to the **Garry**, then runs upstream and under the high road bridge. Take the side-path up on to the bridge for the view of the river, then return to follow the descending path signed 'Pitlochry via Faskally'. This runs down to the bridge.

> **WHAT TO LOOK FOR** ⓘ
>
> Between the two world wars, much of the southern Highlands was developed with small scale hydro-electric schemes. Loch Faskally is artificial, and you'll pass the **Clunie power station**. Its stone arch commemorates the five people who died in the construction of the Clunie Tunnel, which brings water from Loch Tummel. Small hydro schemes do less damage than most forms of energy generation, but there is a price to pay: the Linn of Tummel was the Tummel Falls until it was half-drowned by Loch Faskally.

# The Nevis Gorge and its Waterfalls

*A walk beside Scotland's Himalayan lookalike leading to an enormous waterfall.*

| | |
|---|---|
| •DISTANCE• | 2½ miles (4km) |
| •MINIMUM TIME• | 1hr 30min |
| •ASCENT / GRADIENT• | 270ft (82m) ▲▲ ▲ ▲ |
| •LEVEL OF DIFFICULTY• | 🚶🚶 🚶🚶 🚶🚶 |
| •PATHS• | Well-built path with drops alongside, no stiles |
| •LANDSCAPE• | Deep wooded gorge, wet meadow above |
| •SUGGESTED MAP• | aqua3 OS Explorer 392 Ben Nevis & Fort William |
| •START / FINISH• | Grid reference: NN 168691 |
| •DOG FRIENDLINESS• | Off lead, beware of steep slopes alongside path |
| •PARKING• | Walkers' car park at end of Glen Nevis road |
| •PUBLIC TOILETS• | Glen Nevis Visitor Centre |

## BACKGROUND TO THE WALK

The Nevis Gorge, it's been said, is where Scotland pays its little tribute to the Himalayas. High walls of crag and boulder rise on either side. The path runs through a narrow gap where forest clings to the steep hillside and the river crashes below among its boulders.

### Rocks Galore

Four different types of rock make up this scenery, and three of them are obvious from the walk. The crushed and ancient rocks of the Central Highlands (the Dalradian series) are mostly grey schist, but here there is also the pale-grey quartzite of Sgurr a' Mhaim, above the bend of the glen. The grinding of the continents at the time the Caledonian mountains were formed caused great bubbles of melted rock within the schist. These now appear at the surface as the granite on the lower slopes of Ben Nevis. It's grey on the outside, but pink when freshly broken or washed by streams. The granite was formed deep underground, but above it volcanoes were pouring out the black lava that now forms the summit of Ben Nevis and its formidable northern crags.

### The First Fall

As the glen bends east towards the gorge, stop at the Polldubh car park (grid ref NN 145683). The first waterfall is hidden underneath the road bridge. The riverbed is the pinkish Nevis granite, cut by two dykes – vertical intrusions of volcanic rock – which the river has eroded into twin channels.

Continue up the road to its end at the second car park, where the walk starts. Glen Nevis has the rounded outline of a glacial valley. Glacier-smoothed rock below the car park has become an informal 'symbolic cemetery', commemorating those killed by the mountains they loved. Once above the gorge, the depth of the former glacier is shown by the rocks of Meall Cumhann, on the Ben Nevis (north) side. These are obviously smoothed by the ice that has passed right over the top of them.

**Walk 50**

**Steall Fall**

Steall Fall is about 300ft (91m) high. In a good winter it freezes completely and climbers ascend it in spiked crampons with an ice axe in each hand. The valley above the fall, the Allt Coire a' Mhail, once flowed gently out into a higher version of Glen Nevis. From above, it still appears to unwary walkers to do so. Ice deepened Glen Nevis by 750ft (228m). In the following 10,000 years, the side-stream has barely started its task of eroding the hanging valley down to the level of its new endpoint.

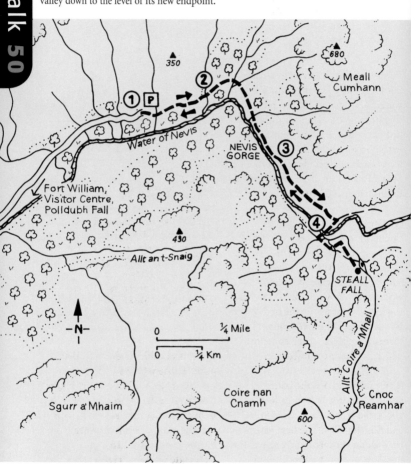

## Walk 50 Directions

① It should be noted that the waterslide above the car park is the **Allt Coire Eoghainn** – if you mistake it for the Steall Fall and set off towards it you are on a difficult and potentially dangerous path. The path you will take on this walk is much easier, but even here there have been casualties, mostly caused by people wearing unsuitable shoes. At the top end of the car park you will see a signpost that shows no destination closer than the 13 miles (21km) to Kinlochleven – accordingly, this walk will be a short out-and-back. The well-made path runs gently uphill under woods of birch and hazel, across what turns into a very steep slope.

Walk 50

For a few steps it becomes a rock-cut ledge, with a step across a waterfall side-stream. The path at this point is on clean pink granite, but you will see a boulder of grey schist beside the path just afterwards. Ahead, the top of the **Steall Fall** can now be seen through the notch of the valley.

② The path continues briefly downhill to cross a second stream; the rock now is schist, with fine zigzag stripes of grey and white. A short rock staircase leads to a wooden balcony section. From here the path is just above the bed of the **Nevis Gorge**. The river runs through huge boulders, some of which bridge it completely.

③ Quite suddenly, the path emerges on to a level meadow above the gorge. Ahead, the Steall Fall fills the view. The best path runs along the left-hand edge of the meadow to a point opposite the waterfall.

④ The walk ends here, beside a footbridge which consists simply of

### WHILE YOU'RE THERE ⓘ
The **Glen Nevis Visitor Centre** (Ionad Nibheis) has a detailed account of the geology and glacial effects that you will see in Glen Nevis and audio-visual displays on the natural history of the area. It also sells postcards and snacks. There are picnic tables where you can watch the walkers coming down from Ben Nevis and wonder which ones got to the top.

three steel cables over a very deep pool. Those who wish to attempt the crossing should note that it gets wobblier in the middle; it's hard to turn round, but the return journey is rather easier. From the wire bridge, the driest path runs alongside the main river round one bend before heading up to the foot of the waterfall. The view from directly beneath is even more spectacular.

### WHAT TO LOOK FOR ⓘ
At Point ②, where the path dips to cross a stream, hot rocks have penetrated cracks in the grey schist to form intrusive **dykes**. Two different ones are visible in the bare rock underfoot. The volcanic rock itself has squeezed into the older schist to form a vein of pink porphyry. Near by, hot magma has vaporised part of the schist itself, and this has recondensed to a vein of whitish quartz. These intrusions are much clearer to see when the rock is wet.

# Acknowledgements

**Front cover:** Loweswater, AA World Travel Library/P Sharpe